UNCLOGGING

THE ANTIDOTE TO OVERWHELM

EVE BROENLAND

"This book delivers such a profound solution to our most common and pressing issue"
Laura van den Berg-Sekac international bestselling author of GET UNSTUCK NOW

UNCLOGGING

THE ANTIDOTE TO OVERWHELM

EVE BROENLAND

Copyright © 2020 Eve Broenland

First Edition

All rights reserved. No part of this publication may be reproduced, stored in, or introduced into a retrieval system, or transmitted, in any form or by any means (electronic, mechanical, photocopying, recording or otherwise), without the prior written permission from the author.

Contact the author:
www.evebroenland.com

Editing by Johanna Leigh
Cover designed by May Phan
Book layout by Marvin Tojos
Illustrations by Nazmul Numan

ISBN: 978-0-6487870-0-6

To mum and dad,

Who will have difficulties reading this as English isn't their first language but will try nonetheless, as they're so supportive. Sorry for always challenging you when you challenged me, but that made me one heck of a determined woman. And sorry for not making you grandparents.

CONTENTS

PART I – PROBLEMS & PRINCIPLES   **7**

    1   WHY THIS BOOK?   9
    2   MY STORY   19
    3   SIMPLICITY   27
    4   WHAT IS UNCLOGGING?   35

PART II – RETHINK   **47**

    5   KNOW YOURSELF   49
    6   ADDING POSITIVITY   75
    7   COMMUNICATE WITH YOURSELF   91

PART III – REDO   **107**

    8   EVALUATE   109
    9   LET GO   119
    10   ACTION   135

PART IV – REVIEW   **153**

    11   STAY UNCLOGGED   155
    12   WHAT'S NEXT   173

PART I
Problems & Principles

1

Why this book?

IT'S FEBRUARY 2019 and I've decided to write my book about unclogging. And before I tell you how I got to this point and why I know it's important for you to know *why* and *how* to unclog, I want to highlight that this writing is at the epitome of my own unclogging. I've removed myself from all distractions, all the things that can stop or block me from succeeding in writing this book. To the people in my life, I mentioned I was going to be unavailable for several days, away from my home, away from my daily commitments, even away from the internet, tv, and all the other things that keep us occupied. Some people referred to it as my writer's retreat. To me it means one thing exclusively and that is **unclogging**; not only have I literally removed myself from these things, it's also the mental aspect of just being here. My head is clear, my mind is open, ideas can come and go, and can freely flow. I don't have to stick to any routine, and there are no expectations for the intended results I have in mind. I will sit here and write, and I know whatever needs to come to light will come to light, as I have nothing else on my mind. It's a slightly daunting idea just sitting here on my own and writing. It's almost like putting my own teachings to the test, to see how well they work.

See, I know that unclogging is essential, for our busy lives, in our busy worlds, and for our busy minds. With all the expectations we put on ourselves, the pressure we feel from the outside, and trapped in the ever-increasing stream of information, technology, and marketing; we need to have a way to navigate through this, so we can feel in control, at ease, clear, and free from struggling. And of course, I know what I'm about to show and explain to you actually works. And I hope with every bone in my body you will be inspired to implement my teachings, or else I wouldn't put in all this effort. I must admit, putting myself to this ultimate test is challenging in a certain way. Hopefully, by the time you hold this book in your hand, we will both know this works. It's now just up to me to get us there. Exciting, hey?

The expectations we put on ourselves

Let me come back to the point I've just made about having no expectations for the desired outcomes I have for writing this book. Having no expectations sounds really simple, but oh, believe me, that doesn't come easily to me. I've always been results focused. Growing up I was a pretty smart cookie and as many others, you get a lot of compliments and praise for doing a good job. The teachers at school, my parents and even I myself would always be happy about a job well done. This perspective invariably became an integral part of me; from primary school all the way through to high school, university and in my corporate job. Working towards the achievement of a goal is human nature and can totally support us, but it's also a limiting factor, which I'll address when I discuss goal setting and reassessing. But think about it, when rewards and achievements are always your main driver and indicator for your happiness, you will constantly be driven to aim higher and how do you ever know when it is enough?

These expectations result in a burdening feeling of pressure. And it's not the same as feeling motivated. Motivation is something originating from within, in alignment with our core beliefs and something that excites us. A goal driven by motivation and intent will support you, but externally driven goals (set by you or the outside world) will feel more like a burden.

You will consequently end up feeling under pressure and obligated to meet those expectations. And if they are in the slightest beyond your capabilities, timeframe or resources, they will contribute hugely to your stress levels. Motivation is positive, expectations never are.

It's now the time to get absolutely clear and real with yourself. What's important to you and what's not? What motivates and drives you and what doesn't? And what is possible and what's not? How to get there? All the answers will be revealed in this book.

We are wired for distractions

The biggest reason for me writing my book in a secluded area where I know I won't be disturbed and distracting myself will be limited, is that we as humans are wired for distractions. It is actually true for most animals but let's move the focus to mammals for the moment. If you are an animal living in the forest and you're happily grazing around, and suddenly you hear a rustling noise behind you, you automatically get into a state of alert; you freeze, your eyes frantically look around and you listen intently. All your senses are focused on this sound that got your attention. It kickstarts your stress responses and your body goes into the freeze, fight or flight mode. This response has kept us alive and is so deeply ingrained in us that our attention always gets drawn towards disturbances. It's indeed extremely helpful should you have been an animal in the forest. And in some vulnerable situations it still is, but with the constant alerts, pop-ups, and notifications from our daily surrounds, it's not in the least helpful for our productivity, concentration or state of mind. Unfortunately, being wired for distractions and coping with it, will require an extra effort from us. And that's the reason I'm writing this book for you and why I'm writing

It's all a matter of how you deal with your environment in a way that works for you.

it away from email, social media, tv, and people. It's however not a requirement having to remove yourself from your normal surroundings. Most of us feel more secure in our familiar surroundings and we love living our lives in the everyday comforts. Emails, messenger, texts, and Facebook do add value to most of us. But not having to deal with those distractions is what's helping the most now. We cannot all go off living in the sticks somewhere and neither do we want to. It's all a matter of how you deal with your environment in a way that works for you. The key is becoming aware of your disruptors, eliminating or managing them and implementing what you know will support you.

Our era of distractions is evident. Constant access through our devices with never-ending streams of information, connections, and options surround us. An average smartphone user picks up their phone 150 times a day and spends about 3 to 5 hours on it. Have you ever noticed yourself scrolling on a social media app when you realise you picked up your phone checking whether you have a spot free in your calendar the coming Friday? I think we all have experienced this, but what we may not realise is how this affects us. It's a common belief that we're losing our attention span, and although focus is essential, that's not the topic of this book nor the concept of unclogging. There is a lot of noise out there, always competing for our attention and it's up to you to find out what is of value and what is not. Unclogging is a process of helping you identify what isn't working for you, to filter out these disruptors and to emphasise what matters most.

Why do we struggle?

Our environment has become a lot more complicated in the last few decades. Presently, over the span of two days, more data is being created than for our entire civilisation up to 2013. We are surrounded by more information, news updates, tailored marketing, technology advancements, and a multitude of options to choose from every day. We live a fast-paced life where the expectation to respond promptly, choose wisely and keep up, are affecting us, consciously or unconsciously. And even more so outside the usual scope of our own internal drive to perform well. Not even mentioning the pressure we feel from our family members, like making our parents proud or being a good role model for our children, and the demands from our immediate environment, such as our boss, our spouse or relatives.

Where we used to write letters and a turnaround of a week or so was absolutely acceptable, we now all have smartphones, so why not respond within an hour to a text message or any other request? This combined with the increasing amount of information and options, leaves us clueless as to how to process this overload of input. Better yet, even though we think we can, we actually aren't able to process all this information and decision fatigue (a poor-quality decision due to making too many decisions and weighing them all up) is a real thing. Our brains cannot deal with this overload of information and results in us feeling overwhelmed and confused, sometimes even anxious. Research tells us that the brain receives 11 million pieces of information per second but only has the ability to process 40 pieces per second. The information surrounding us is overburdening to process and we either need to eliminate it or have very clear filters in place that work for us on an individual level. Noise for you might not be noise for others, but it's important to distinguish what your disruptors are.

Finally, an ever-prevalent and visible environment, especially the use of social media, further aggravates our struggle. One of the biggest culprits is the feeling that we need to keep up and if you're not clear about what's important to you, it can lead to the comparison trap. Seeing others posting images of their amazing lives across social media, might make you feel inadequate and insecure. Another very important aspect of the unclogging journey is to identify whether your goals and actions truly reflect who you are or if you are following other people's or society's expectations, norms, and standards.

WHY THIS BOOK?

An imbalanced life

With our fast-paced environment, life's soaring demands and our own high expectations, it is no wonder we all feel so busy. We glorify being busy, it seems to be the standard. When asking people how they've been, nine out of ten people respond with the reply 'busy'. We're being raised with the belief that we have to work super hard. It's alarming that we're also losing the ability to do nothing as we even want to be 'productive' during our leisure time. We want to make the most of everything. And although I highly appreciate the drive for efficiency, it's evident this isn't working well for us. Our minds are always 'on', our to-do lists are never-ending, and we never have enough hours in the day. We're not switching off and the toll it has on us is obvious. We feel stressed, confused and overwhelmed, we tend to react irritated, defensive and frustrated, and our enjoyment of life is reduced as we continue to struggle.

Think of an ecosystem, let's take a forest as an example. When the forest is flourishing, it's able to develop, regenerate and manage disturbances. Trees grow and appear healthy, there's undergrowth and all species in the food web support one another. However, if this system is disrupted by for example newly introduced species, removal of species or even when abnormal changes in temperatures or rainfalls are too significant or long-lasting, the system will not be able to cope. It will fall out of balance.

The same goes for our own environment. Too many outside influences will affect our own systems as well as our habitats. It causes an imbalance. The easiest way to explain this is through your body. Your body functions on two systems. The sympathetic nervous system is your active system, adrenaline kicks in, energy is being used and stress responses are also triggered. The parasympathetic nervous system is your rest and digest system, where you restore your energy reserves. When your body is constantly stimulated by these external influences or an overly busy mind, your body endures stress. Your stress response requires the use of hormones like adrenaline and this leads to lowered energy levels. If this stress response is triggered too often or for too long, your system will fatigue. And this leads to a lower immune system because your body doesn't have time to recover; hence stress being the biggest risk factor in human health these days. When adrenaline levels are completely depleted, it can even lead to burnout.

The same principle that applies to the forest applies to you; a system that is out of balance doesn't flourish. To manage your disruptions, the changes, and the demands, it's vital you manage your system properly. You just need to know how.

Going back to our habit of busyness; have you ever wondered why you are so busy or you're feeling busier than ever? Data shows that our working hours have flatlined in the last decades to about 40 hours a week and time spent on household chores has significantly reduced through our advancing technologies. Quantitatively we're not busier, but qualitatively we are. With all the options available and being able to be distracted so easily, it is no wonder our minds can't keep up. It's exhausting. But you can equip yourself with the necessary tools to manage this. It starts here. And it goes beyond coping mechanisms, as those are only temporary measures. We'll be working towards a sustainable system that works for you, to make you the one in control, rather than your environment controlling you.

I'm excited to dive into this with you so you are aware of what's going on and how you can equip yourself to manage all these disturbances. It's polluting your environment; it's draining your energy, and it's making life difficult. It's time to do it differently, manage yourself and be in control. It's time to unclog.

What will this book give you?

When life gets confusing and overwhelming, it's time to take a step back and utilise the power of elimination. There's only one way to do this and that's by simplifying your surroundings. Once done, your options will be reduced, and this will provide you with the clarity you need. But this is a skill we're not familiar with. Letting go, rather than pushing through is the way to deal with everything surrounding you. And that's exactly what I'm here for.

I've coached many of my clients on tools to make their lives less complicated. To implement this, we need to learn how to let go, understand what's most important to us and know what works for us. It's almost contradicting to instil limitations through elimination that is geared toward more freedom and happiness. But you'll soon understand it is the only way to restore the balance; to feel good, calm and happy.

Firstly, we'll dive into the concepts and then the tools. PART I describes in more detail how our environment is affecting us, why you're clogged and how the three-step process of unclogging will work to simplify your life. PART II outlines the first step; **rethink,** where you get to understand yourself better, the most important thing you can do for yourself. You'll learn why and how to add more positivity in your life and how to start communicating with yourself on a daily basis for more clarity. PART III focuses on different actions; **redo** is the second step of the unclogging cycle. In this step, you'll be able to put into practice everything you know about yourself. We'll evaluate your goals and you'll get a full reality check, followed by the steps to let go and take action. PART IV is the completion of the cycle where you'll learn to constantly **review** what supports you and what works for you. There is no point in putting in all the hard work and then not knowing how to proceed when things become challenging again. This final step really prepares you for the future, through the building of your personal resilience and the ability to manage your system.

I'd suggest you take a highlighter pen and mark the specific sections you think would work for you. To make it even easier for you every chapter finishes with the key points and suggestions for you on how to implement the concepts of the chapter. It's my goal that you'll be able to straight away implement what you've learned but that you'll also find your unique toolbox of the things that work for you.

Who is this book for?

If I've done my job well you've picked up this book because you feel there's too much going on in your life and at times it's making you feel overwhelmed, stressed, and unsure. You want to know how to better cope with this and you haven't been able to figure out why you feel this way. Even if you've read other books about this, you're not entirely sure how to implement this and you feel stuck and frustrated. You're a rational being I'm thus going to give you facts. And since you're a pragmatic person who wants to live a more exciting life, to do so you need tools that are easily implementable. Although you might feel a bit unsure, you're ready for a change. Because you know somewhere down the line something has got to give. Life doesn't have to be this overwhelming. Let's unclog together.

My promise to you

I'm not going to be your buddy, I'm going to be your coach. I'm going to support, challenge and guide you. You have a circle of good friends who are great for support, but I guess you're reading this because you want a bit more. You want to get more out of this life, you want to progress, and currently you feel stuck. And a buddy-buddy approach from my end isn't going to get you there. We are going to get downright honest with each other, really dig deeper into what's holding you back and also uncover all the excuses you make for yourself.

I will say this though; I applaud you for making this start. And that's coming straight from my heart! Everything that you'll read in this book is going to be one hundred percent honest and sincere. But I want to let you know that it's really amazing you're here. You're ready for a change, without the BS, without the excuses. You're adamant to start living this amazing life of yours. You're brave, bold and beautiful for making this start. Big applause to you!

And it's ok being scared, or at least slightly apprehensive. That's just the unknown playing games with your mind. I totally get it; this book thing is scary for me too. But I feel supported and I'll help you feel supported too. We've got this!

What else can you expect from me besides my total honesty? I'm here with love, as only love supports change. The opposite of the coin is fear and it's exactly that fear that keeps you stuck in the same place. But love is not all rainbows, butterflies, and chardonnay in the park. If you truly want this, there's some work in store for you. But that also means results, yay!

I promise you I'll keep it simple. I don't want to add more pressure to your life. I want to give you the insight to understand why this is important. I want to equip you with the practical and implementable tools that will enable you to let go, make things less complicated and feel in control of your environment. And that is exactly what unclogging will do.

I want to take you on a journey with this book. It'll be your pathway to increased awareness and simplicity; enabling you to live your life with more clarity, confidence, and contentment. It has the potential to elevate your quality of life in a more significant way you can ever imagine. It's my duty and desire to teach you how and then it's up to you to implement my teachings. As one of my valued mentors once said to me 'knowledge is worthless if you don't put it into practice'. Hence I'm counting on you to implement what you learn here en route toward that amazing life of yours!

2

My story

Living simply

My first childhood memory is sitting in the early summer morning with a white cute girly bucket next to my dad who's turning over the soil in the large vegetable patch we owned. Equipped with his spade, he's pushing the blade of the spade into the muddy soil with his clog while I sit next to him watching him work. As soon as the moist soil is turned over, I see earthworms poking out. I grab them with my bare hands and put them in my bucket. And once I have a few earthworms; I wander over to the back of our block behind the shed where we have our chook pen and feed the worms to our chickens. I watch my mum attending to the laundry, the plants or fruit bushes and I happily wander back to join my dad again.

Growing up in a small and slightly rural town in The Netherlands with my loving parents and 18 months older brother, life was pretty simple and normal. My parents have been married for almost 50 years and watching them growing old together makes me realise there's nothing more I want than that. On my own wedding day in 2007, our photographer was able to capture a cheeky shot of them where my mum was nibbling my dad's ear. They love and adore each other to the ends of the earth. But of course, every upbringing comes with challenges and for us, it was dealing with an above average household intelligence level. My dad is very rational and extremely smart. Needless to mention that everything that had to get past him had to be explained with sound arguments based on facts and figures. To get my way, I learned very quickly to do my research and be very argumentative. Funnily enough, my dad never wanted to have kids, he loved his life the way it was. I have that from him, that combined with a relentless determination. My mum is extremely caring and was always around while I was growing up. As a profound role model in my life, she gifted me with a fantastic mix of household management skills and feminine independence. She instilled the desire in me to have a tidy home, prepare delicious and nutritious meals and care for others and animals. My brother is more of an introvert, and he no doubts inherited the intellectual gene from my dad. Like any other parents, our parents wanted us to perform well in life, especially because we were both smart and quick learners. They didn't want us to waste our potentials and always encouraged us one hundred percent.

Being a bright student but with sass and determination; perhaps also a bit of youthful idealism, at the age of 14, I've already set myself the goal to study marine biology. And not a single career orientation day at school would make me change my mind. I did just that, and at 23 I got my Master's Degree in marine biology, but I noticed a gap I wanted to fill. A pure science degree, as I just completed, was less practical, and as I was looking for something with more applicable aspects, I completed my second Master's Degree in environmental science a year and a half later. Always paddling my own canoe, and constantly aiming higher and higher to achieve success, I got married straight out of university. It made sense and it was nice to start our lives together this way. My husband Frank and I ended up travelling in Australia where I landed my first job as the environmental advisor for a salt mine. It is worth mentioning that it was on the stunning Western Australia coastline in a World Heritage Area.

For four years we lived a very modest life in a very remote town with only around one hundred residents, all people who worked for the company. Our colleagues were our neighbours, our friends, and our community. On evenings and weekends, most of us went fishing, camping or chilling on the beach. Our commute to work was a three-minute drive while at the same time having the privilege of spotting amazing types of wildlife; dolphins, turtles, dugongs, sea snakes, rays, and many majestic bird species were spotted on frequent occasions. The weekly truck delivered our grocery supplies and my planning skills came in very handy here. But we also learned to be totally okay with asking and sharing when not having a certain item close at hand. I remember one of my friends going around town one evening searching for pineapple when she wanted to make sweet and sour pork but she had forgotten to order a can of pineapple. After about eight attempts she knocked on my door and I happened to have a fresh pineapple in the house for her.

So yes, life was very simple and uncomplicated, and I loved it. There was no need to lock our doors. Besides nature there was nowhere we could go, nor anywhere we needed to be. And the company provided accommodation and utilities with the result that we pretty much had nothing to worry about.

Four years later when the company promoted me to an environmental manager, we moved to Perth. It was a fantastic opportunity for us as I was ready to continue to learn. Living in such a unique and remote part of the world was an absolute privilege that I would never take for granted and that I will always cherish; simple, beautiful, and serene. Even though I could've lived there for the rest of my life, I guess it was time to move on.

How I got clogged

We took it easy to adapt to suburban living in Perth. Perth is the capital of Western Australia and although it's the most casual city of Australia, it certainly is a lot busier than a remote town. Of course, we now had to sort out the usual; a roof over our heads, a vehicle, utilities, insurances, sports, groceries, and a new daily routine including the city commute. For both of us work went well, but nothing exciting or ground-breaking. Our social circle grew, and we loved spending time with our friends. Or just the two of us spending quality time at home with our two dogs, over a glass of wine or two. My husband was also able to fulfil his lifelong dream; we started a martial arts school, running four classes a week outside our usual working hours.

But without realising it, this all had a huge effect on me. I would suddenly find myself in tears over weekends or during my morning commutes to work. I would feel lost, overwhelmed and confused. Why was I suddenly so unhappy? Everything was in place and going well.

I can remember this one Sunday afternoon; after finishing all the household tasks, the social obligations and the administration for the martial arts school, I finally sat down and had time for myself. With me, I had my iPad with an episode I wanted to watch, my digital SLR camera with a few tutorials I still needed to go through, two books I was reading without making real progress, my red nail polish to do my toe nails, and a Dutch magazine a friend gave to me to read. How on earth did I think I could do all those things within the next two hours before it would be dinner prep time? Instead of looking forward to a couple of hours of unwinding me-time, I put pressure on myself by wanting to do too much and feeling totally overwhelmed. But these were my favourite hobbies and I either wanted to do too much or didn't have enough time.

As these meltdown moments became more frequent, I referred to them as my 'mood swings' as I had no idea why I suddenly felt so unhappy and I made an appointment with a naturopath. I put these moments down to possible hormonal changes and hoped the naturopath could help me. It was Wednesday 6th of March 2014, a day before I turned 32. I am welcomed and greeted with a warm smile and without any judgement she's asking about me: *"What do you do?" "Why are you here?"* and *"What's going on?"* And apart from the repetitive mood swings, I tell her that my life is great. I've got a wonderful husband, I love my house and my dogs, I've got a well-paying job in a field I've studied seven years for and am super proud of, and I've got friends and family that love and support me. But about 20 minutes into the conversation she looks me in the eye and asks me; "*Who would you be if we would strip away all those achievements?*"

I was totally caught off guard. I didn't know how or what to answer and tears started running down my face. Her question left me speechless as I've been focusing on the output, the achievements, my entire life. It brought me to the harsh realisation that my environment could never make me happy. All I've worked so very hard for was great and made me feel proud, but it was not going to bring about the fulfilment in my life I so longed for. Now was the time letting go of the pressure I brought on myself and reducing the overwhelm from my world. And here's what I did and what I realised:

How I got unclogged

The first step I took, was to set aside more time for myself, more me-time. I toyed with the idea of cutting down my working days by one day every fortnight and taking a pay cut. Even though very comfortable with our income, I was quite aware that the reducing of my hours would also mean getting paid less every month. But I asked myself the question: "*What advice would I give to my best friend if she presented me with this dilemma?*" And it actually was surprisingly easy; why would I not want my friend to feel happier and less stressed? There and then I followed my own advice (always helpful by the way) and it made it a very easy decision.

I made an effort to spend more time reading. I stumbled on a few blogs (one being ZenHabits from Leo Babauta) mainly on concepts of changing habits and minimalism; which is the principle to live your life with less. It was so intrigued and inspired that I went through my entire household in a systematic way to reduce my belongings. I started very simple; getting rid of junk gathered over time but serving no purpose, and that we didn't need. Next, I ditched the clothing and jewellery I hardly ever wore, my old make-up and the kitchen items I almost never used. The third round was more challenging, but it didn't stop me in my tracks, and

I continued on my mission. I liked the idea of challenging myself to see what would happen if I got rid of more stuff. This third round involved discarding more valuable items like a pair of super modern glasses that always gave me a headache after a day of wearing them, but I kept them out of guilt having spent a significant amount of money on them. Then I tossed out some shoes that actually didn't match anything and were impractical, but oh so pretty.

At one point I laid out my digital SLR camera on our glass dining table with all the lenses and other accessories I've collected. My husband was walking past as I was taking photos of it with my phone, asking me with astonishment; *"Are you really getting rid of that?"* I'm confident he didn't realise he challenged me at that moment as I wasn't a hundred percent sure myself. I loved taking photos, I was a good photographer, and it was a very good camera (for Nikon lovers, it was the D7000). But it was heavy and not entirely practical. And although I really tried putting in an effort to learn all the ins and outs, I didn't completely master all the features. And not mentioning the collection of digital photos I still needed to sort through. To be honest, beside our last oversees holiday I didn't touch the camera for two years. To use it actually became more of a burden for me rather than something I loved. I sold it second-hand for a snippet of what I paid for it. Since then I just used my mobile phone. I could've kept the camera as it wasn't in the way, but I always felt pressured and obliged to use it. I felt heavy and made me feel slightly guilty, looking at it when opening the cabinet. There have only been a few moments I wish I still had it, but it never weighed up against the release I felt after getting rid of that pressure.

I also committed more time to my yoga practice, one that went way beyond the poses on the mat. Yoga philosophies intrigued me, and I went on a yoga retreat and a few years later to India for yoga teacher training with a traditional teacher. Yoga, as does martial arts, is something I live by every day. It's the discipline and the means of connecting to myself that supports me.

After attending a yoga and mindfulness workshop, I realised how much I was missing studying. But instead of going for another degree (I was contemplating naturopathy, but I couldn't see myself fully committing to a formal study that I wasn't sure I was going to use in the future) I committed to studying one self-development book every month for a year. And I did this with diligence; I read the entire book, took notes, wrote up a summary, provided a presentation to my husband and compiled a list of actionable items to ensure I could implement what I've learned to see if it worked for me or not. This commitment, although not realising it at the time, was the start of something bigger, which you're now holding a copy of.

The big payoff of all this, was the beginning of understanding what was and wasn't working for me. I changed things around and then reflected on the results. I grew to better understand myself and applied what I've learned. It gave me clarity, calmness and a feeling of being in control. My life became easier, less hectic and by all means less overwhelming.

I continued learning; I studied positive psychology, many self-development books, and eastern philosophy. And I collectively combined my experiences, my core beliefs and my knowledge into what is now the concept of unclogging; the three-step process to being able to navigate through life with ease, as the antidote to overwhelm. The concept shows you how to identify, manage, and eliminate disruptors so you can take control of your environment. And it's absolutely possible for you to get there too. It will require your commitment and a dose of determination, but once you've started (always the hard part in my opinion) you'll see how it will give you clarity and help to make your life simple.

3

Simplicity

---

*"Life is really simple, but we insist
on making it complicated."*
— Confucius

*"The secret of happiness is not found in seeking more,
but in developing the capacity to enjoy less."*
— Socrates

"Simplicity is the ultimate sophistication."
— Leonardo Da Vinci

IF YOU THINK that living simply is the latest hype, then the above quotes from very intelligent men from our history show that it's always been a challenge for us. But we can also conclude that it is essential to strive for simplicity. A simple life is a happy life.

We do make things too complicated for ourselves and that's mainly caused by our minds being distracted so easily. And in our current society, this becomes even more relevant by the amount of information and options surrounding us. Of course, some technological advancements do make our lives easier, but it undeniably adds to our overwhelm by the exponential increase of available options. Historical trends show that employee output per hour has doubled every 35 years and we currently read the equivalent of 170 newspapers a day. How can we keep up with information consumption at this rate?

Going forward we need to make things simpler for ourselves. There's no way our brains can adapt to the same rate as the amount of data surrounding us, the demands put on us and the goals we set for ourselves. We already see many companies simplifying the customer experience and aiming to better streamline their processes. It's now time for us to apply this to our own lives. We owe it to ourselves to make life less complicated.

The source of happiness

Simplicity is the source of happiness. It's that simple.

Let me explain. What does simplicity involve? It requires you focusing on the most important aspects; the essence, the core, the foundation, whether applying it to your home, work, goals, relationships or organisation. Doing so, brings about clarity and self-awareness. It highlights what's important to you and finally presents you with the opportunity of self-acceptance. By letting go of what doesn't represent you (anymore), you are gaining clarity. That automatically provides you with confidence as it now becomes easier to make decisions aligning with who you are and what you believe in.

For me, I realised that my unhappiness at work stemmed from the goals I set for myself at the age of 14 and they were no longer serving me. That realisation supported me in easily accepting my redundancy at work a year later. I took it as a huge opportunity, a chance to readjust and make sure I found something that aligns with me. That doesn't mean everyone has to quit their job, but it's an example of accepting what wasn't working for me. Through my increased self-awareness I was able to take the next step with more ease.

Simplicity additionally presents you with the opportunity to build confidence, compassion, and contentment. These three C's will be your outcomes throughout this book as you gain a better understanding of the principle of unclogging and what it can do for you. When identifying what's disrupting you and exercising the power of elimination, you're gaining an unbelievable amount of clarity. Confusion fizzles out and makes way for **confidence**. While learning to better understand what works for you and what doesn't and how your system best functions, you'll also come to realise that this doesn't necessarily apply to others. Understanding the perspective of other people is the foundation of **compassion**. And lastly, when accepting and letting go of what isn't serving you, you'll notice a sense of calm and **contentment** growing in you. Your expectations decrease and you'll be ok with what and how things are. This is acceptance.

By being able to accept yourself, be content with your surroundings, understand others and be clear in what works for you, you will be happy.

A means to be in control

Simplifying also equips you with the tools to be in control, and here we're dealing with the 4th C. It's impossible to control everything happening in your life, and it's important to realise that. But the things we can control, are the same things we can simplify. Take for instance your family life; you can control how you spend your time with your loved ones, but you can't control unfortunate events from happening. You can scale down on your hobbies and have more time to enjoy them. The final decision is yours and that's what gives you the control. Sometimes these decisions are challenging, and we'd prefer to not make them. But ultimately, it's still up to you to find out what works for you and to then put that into action.

Why do we want to be in control?

Feeling in control is one of our basic needs. As Maslow's hierarchy of needs describes so well, that the first and second level of our desired needs is stability; we want to feel we have the aspects of food and shelter sorted out and under control. As humans, we like a dose of variety, but if everything was unknown, we would feel very lost and confused, which is precisely what's happening with us right now, living in an ever-changing environment. Being in control also makes room for peace, calmness, and clarity. The simple act of putting things away after use immediately creates a sense of control. It makes your environment tidier and things are easier to find when you need them again.

At home, I make a point of ensuring everything has its place and after use, I put it back in the same place. This way all my surface areas are always clean, and nothing is just 'laying around'. It requires a certain degree of discipline, but I never have to waste time trying to find something and cleaning is a breeze. It's consistent, efficient and sustainable. Having things in order gives the same sense of control. I'm in control of my home environment and I give it the respect it deserves. It's not chaos, it's clear. It doesn't overwhelm, it's a calm space.

Being consistent, feeling in control and making your own decisions, is also at the cornerstone of your happiness. You're in control of your environment rather than your environment controlling you. Knowing that our environment, as described earlier on, can be hugely overwhelming, it's important to protect yourself against it. By making sure you're managing it properly, is the start of an easier and more simple life.

Feeling pressure or feeling clear

If you look at the diagram below you see four different layers. The centre is who you are. The second layer is what you think and feel; your rational and emotional self. The next layer is what you do and say; your actions and how you interact with the world. The most outside layer is what you surround yourself with.

You now have two ways you can go through life; one way is to work from the outside in, the other is from the inside out. If you let your environment, what you've surrounded yourself with, dictate how you act and respond which then affects how you think and feel, who you are or how you perceive yourself, it's not aligning with yourself and results in you feeling stressed and unhappy. This is the pressure we feel from society, which then results in the expectations we put on ourselves.

The other way is working from the inside out. If you're clear on who you are and being aware of your thoughts and emotions, which then culminates in how you interact with your environment and ultimately how your environment is being shaped, it's in alignment with yourself. It's giving you clarity and control, and it makes it so much easier to deal with everything that comes your way. You'll have more confidence, as you now have the clarity to know what works for you and what doesn't.

Here's how it played out for one of my clients, her name is Carolyn. Carolyn worked as a senior associate at a law firm and felt really exhausted. She's fantastic at her job, conforms to deadlines and is always ready to help. A great combination you'd say, but for Carolyn, it meant that everyone always ran to her asking for help with finishing agreements and she never said no. This made her feel very tired as she was helping everyone first before starting to work on her own tasks. There were many days she was working till midnight or even longer and the next day she was exhausted before the day even started. During our coaching sessions, she came to the understanding that she was led by her environment and we started to work from the inside out. Carolyn didn't have a lot of confidence, but as soon as she got to know herself better, the confidence emerged as a logical result. She was able to figure out what she needed each day, and was also able to communicate that to her colleagues. She still loved helping others, but it was no longer going to be to the detriment of her own work. She set her boundaries while still being able to help others. It wasn't a magic fix, and there were still some long days at the office, but she was aware which relieved her of the constant pressure. And after her long days at work she now also had the tools to recover, adjust and continue. She was able to align her actions with who she is, rather than the reverse. She was in control and she was able to adjust her situation in a way that worked for her.

> **She was in control and she was able to adjust her situation in a way that worked for her.**

Assumptions about simplicity

One of the biggest assumptions people make and use as validation and objection to a simple life, is that they love being busy and thrive on an active life. I had a client who never wanted her life being viewed as simple, she was thriving on challenges. Yet she needed coaching as she didn't have enough time for her children.

A simple life is most definitely not about NOT being challenged or a stagnating personal growth. Believe me, it presents you with abundant challenges and growth. Letting go of goals, beliefs, and habits you've been holding onto for years will for sure test you. Eliminating is so much harder than adding. Simplicity is not easy.

There are most definitely people that are okay with working long hours, but if you're complaining about it or it's affecting you negatively in any way, then you have to be real with yourself and act on it. Your system will tell you; are you tired, restless, or often sick? Make an observation of yourself. Are there any indications that it is or isn't working for you? Are you drinking too much coffee? Do you feel tired as soon as you wake up? If you are struggling with everything that's going on in your life and you want things to be different; the way to get there is by simplifying, and the tool you have to put to work is unclogging.

Unclogging as a tool for a simple life

Unclogging is more than just decluttering or minimalising. It's a holistic approach helping you to understand who you are, what's important to you and being able to implement it in a way that works for you. It's not a cookie cutter approach, it's trial and error, it's a journey, it's up to you to find out what you need.

It's a reality check, like holding up a mirror in front of yourself. It's a process of finding out where things get complicated for you and then having the tools to eliminate, filter or adapt to make life easier, more in flow and in control. It's time to stop feeling overwhelmed, stressed out and unsure. You can wake up every day feeling excited rather than tired, burdened and busy.

Unclogging is a simple three-step process that will help you manage your life and prepare you for the future and every day ahead.

4

What is unclogging?

———

UNCLOGGING IS THE process of becoming aware of what's blocking you and doing something about it. It requires action and commitment, in tandem with learning and adaptability. It's having a set of personal problem-solving skills and being able to apply them. It's taking ownership of your life; from what's going on in your mind to what you're surrounding yourself with. It's you taking ownership of your life and knowing how to navigate, rather than let the world dictate the course of your life. It uncovers the flow of life, new possibilities, opportunities, and experiences. Mostly it's about being able to live your life your way; to be in control, feel excited and at ease.

Unclogging is a lifestyle, not a quick fix. If you think this book will be your magic wand, I truly wish it could be, but that's not how it works. As with all the clients I work with; I tell them upfront they need to put in the work and the same applies here.

WHAT IS UNCLOGGING?

Think about your life as a drain, but things get in the way. Instead of the water draining easily, it might slow down a bit, or it might not be affected at all, or at least so it seems. Some items can be big and bulky and easy to remove, or it might be minuscule or greasy and gets stuck further down. We all have things getting in the way; annoying colleagues, getting sick, an overdue bill, fights with our spouse, or car trouble to name a few. These are the things we usually don't have control over, but they need sorting out. If we don't and we ignore them for a while, things can eventually get really blocked. It's up to you to ensure your drain is clear and unblocked, and when issues beyond your control come in the way, you are equipped to deal with them. But you then have a head start; if your drain is already clear, it's easier to identify the issue and it doesn't affect you as much.

Now think of what you do when your kitchen sink gets clogged up; you first try to drain it, you want the water to run through. Then you might poke at it to try and unblock it. If that works, great. But if it doesn't, you go and research what else you can do. You then try again, but now equipped with more information. This works a bit, yay! But unfortunately for you, it clogs up again. It's now time to find a solution elsewhere; you might need to get some tools, or chemicals or perhaps some advice from someone or YouTube. Finally, the sink starts draining, and it works well for a while. But if you have very challenging blockages that you can't identify at first glance, the drain is going to clog up again. Now you'd most likely have to get a plumber, or you might be fortunate enough to have a handy neighbour. The issues at hand might be sorted out, but no matter at what stage of the process your kitchen sink started flowing again, it's up to you to maintain it and keep it unclogged. Are you perhaps not mindlessly flushing everything down the drain not thinking about the possible effects? Do you have a strainer installed? Or do you have a plunger or unclogging chemicals available for emergencies?

It's time to find out how to take care of your drain. What clogs you up and what allows you to flow? What issues are you having and how are you dealing with them? How can you prepare yourself for them or even have preventative measures in place? And how can you make it all easier for yourself?

Why are we clogged?

I know you like facts so let's dive into more details to find out why we are clogged. Being clogged, as per the drain analogy, is having no real awareness or control over the issues affecting you. This happens when you are operating from the outside in; you let your environment control you. How does this happen?

Our environment

Our environment as briefly mentioned in Chapter 1 undeniably has a huge effect on us. As a society, we've now created 30 exabytes (that's a three with 20 zeros) pieces of human made information and it's growing exponentially. We now create more data every two days than we did for our entire civilisation up to 2013. Think of the high number of news articles getting shared online or tv, or posts on social media sites like Facebook, Instagram, and Twitter. It's impossible to keep up. Just think of the overload of information we consume now compared to two or three decades ago. It all moves much faster and it's everywhere.

Companies continue investing significant percentages of their profits in research and product development. They continue providing us with a multitude of options that we never realised we needed. Supermarkets on average now carry 42,000 different products. Take Head & Shoulders in Australia, they currently provide 27 different options of shampoos and conditioners and in the USA the same company provides a choice of 61 different options. It makes one wonder if this means the Americans now have better hair than the Aussies. And coffee magnet Starbucks proudly advertises an option of 80,000 different combinations of drinks. How are you even able to make a decision?

Marketing is everywhere and it's not limited to your supermarket or newspaper anymore, it pops up on your Facebook feed, your inbox, text messages and is highly personalised. No wonder we sometimes feel we are never enough. Corporations spend $171 billion in advertising, not because they hope they will influence you but because they know they will influence you. It's of vital importance to know how to navigate through all this information and being able to make the decisions that work for you.

How do we process this overload of information? Well, actually we don't. This overbearing load of information and multitude of options leads to two things: decision paralysis and disappointment. As Barry Schwartz wonderfully puts in his very popular TED talk, we end up stepping away from making a choice. An experiment at a supermarket showed when faced with sampling 27 different kinds of jams to opposed to 9 kinds of jam, people were more likely to buy a jam from the stand with the lesser amount of options.

Schwartz also outlines in the same talk, even if we were able to make a choice, we likely end up being disappointed. If the options provided to us are more limited, we're happier with the option we decide on. He uses a personal example of the huge different styles of jeans we can now choose from. While in his earlier years Schwartz only had a handful of jeans to choose from, he recently had to buy a new pair and was stunned by the number of options available. He really just wanted a simple option; the right colour, right size, and a reasonable price. He ended up buying a pair, but with the more options to choose from, he did wonder whether the other style may have been a better choice.

Research from Sheena Iyengar emphasises this effect in her book *The Art of Choosing*. It's very hard to be fully satisfied with the decision you've made when you've opted for a choice in the overwhelming selection. How would you then not reason the other option could've been better? Because of the multitude of options, the risk of comparing it to an option you haven't chosen is plausible. I was in Starbucks in Sydney a few weeks ago and wondering; should I have gone for the gingerbread caramel iced latte instead of the green tea frappuccino? Sounds ridiculous right?

We constantly use the external as a measure for our needs and desires; your clothes are perfectly fine until you attend a higher-social economic function and suddenly you're detecting the flaws in your outfit. Your phone is working fine until Apple comes out with a new one; all of a sudden you decide your photos don't have the desired quality. With the options surrounding us, it's challenging to be satisfied, but it's equally challenging to find out whether it's your own real desire or more of a cultural norm or habit that you're using as measurement. I got myself a new iPhone last year, and until this day I still can't pinpoint whether I really wanted a new phone or whether it was because of the new features that were cool to have.

It's logical that our culture has a huge effect on how we see ourselves. But we can't keep adjusting ourselves to our environment. Yes, it's essential to adapt, but this only works if you know at the core of your being who you are and what's important to you. Only then will you know if upgrading your technology or wardrobe adds value to you.

Let's go back to the ecosystem example and try to see the forest for the trees. If a growing tree would constantly adapt to its environment, it would never become a solid and grounded specimen. It first shoots roots, grows leaves to the sky and it'll do it's best to compete in taking up its space. We absolutely need to be able to adapt, as this will provide us with the resilience to thrive in our environment, and the same goes for the tree. But first of all, we need to be grounded, we need a stable foundation to grow from, and only then can we can deal with all the external influences.

Our mind

Our mind is the other contributor to us feeling overwhelmed. When we have no awareness of what's going on in our minds and our thoughts, our minds can go in overdrive. Every thought that pops up in our head leads us to another thought or action. And if you're not conscious of this, it becomes very challenging to deal with it.

Combine this with our results-focused mindset, and constantly chasing the next goal or next outcome, it results in us being constantly busy, always on the go and feeling like it's a never-ending cycle. Our externally focused mindset relates to the high expectations we set for ourselves and never feeling we're good enough. We get frustrated with ourselves and then try and fix the situation by setting even more and higher goals. It was exactly what I experienced when I wasn't happy during the years I worked in corporate Perth. The only thing I knew was looking at my life with my focus on achievements. The only way I could see me 'fixing' the situation was by setting more goals which put even more pressure on me. It really felt like I was stuck.

By force of habit we've learned to respond straight away; as a child, with our phones, and with our work emails and requests now that we're available 24/7. This too keeps our minds constantly active. And some research even indicates that our attention span has reduced significantly as we're constantly affected by external inputs that the mind has to process.

I had this lovely client, her name is Lizabeth. She always woke up with the feeling that her to-do-list was never ending and she only went to bed after she finished most of her chores. Her mind was constantly busy and sometimes even in overdrive. In these moments she felt extremely stressed and overwhelmed. One of the things she aimed to work on was her mental and physical health. It was, of course, a great goal she set for herself to enable her to take better care of herself and feel good. But like we all tend to do; she straightaway went into action mode after we've established the goal. She was just going to eat healthier, prepare her meals on time, go to Pilates three times a week, wake up earlier, walk the dog every day and start running. Wow, talking about putting the pressure on! But this is how most of us are inclined to approach our situations. As you can understand, this is not helping in reducing the overwhelm. We are so focused on 'more' in life, but we don't have a clue what's really causing all this pressure in the first place.

Why is it important to unclog?

There's no rule that says you have to unclog, but if you want to feel more at ease and in control then I'd say keep reading. If you're honest with yourself and everything is going well for you, I'm utterly happy for you. But it makes me wonder why you picked up this book.

Now that you have an understanding of why we get clogged; through our environment and our mind; and you realise that's why you feel overwhelmed, busy and sometimes unsettled; we can start working to unclog. We can find ways to get rid of the issues once we identify them or filter out the noise around us to make it easier for us to navigate through this. It's a process of uncovering and building on what works for you. And that sounds really simple right, but there's a big reason why that's not working for you yet. It's because we are inclined to sabotage ourselves.

Do you know that the French word for clog is 'sabot'? It stems from the industrialisation era when Dutch woodworkers put chunks of wood 'clogs' in the machines that their employers purchased to replace them as workers. They literally sabotaged the machines so they could keep their jobs.

> **It's a process of uncovering and building on what works for you.**

We sabotage ourselves as we stick our heads in the sand. We don't know what's important to us. We don't align our actions from within. We don't live by our values. We keep trying to fix ourselves, or worse, fix others. We're not aware of how our environment is affecting us. And we don't know how our minds work and how to utilise them better. We are busy most of the time, we don't know where to start and change seems just a little bit too hard.

We sabotage ourselves by not dealing with our environment in a way that works for us. We keep pushing and probing and hoping it all starts flowing again. It's time to get to the core and put in the work to understand what's most important to us. That way we can work from the inside out, gain the necessary clarity and take control of our lives. Promise me one thing, the very first thing you'll do after reading this section is scheduling a specific time for you, at least once a week, but ideally once a day. This small but important step will set the way for bigger changes coming.

Unfortunately, we are never taught how to achieve this personal clarity—how is it then at all possible for us living simple and feeling in control of everything that's going on?

Clogged vs unclogged

There are two ways you can operate; clogged or unclogged. The cycle that you're in when you're clogged is as follows; there's too much surrounding you, there are no clear boundaries or awareness, you set high expectations of yourself, resulting in no joy and feeling stuck like a rat in a wheel.

And this is the reason why:

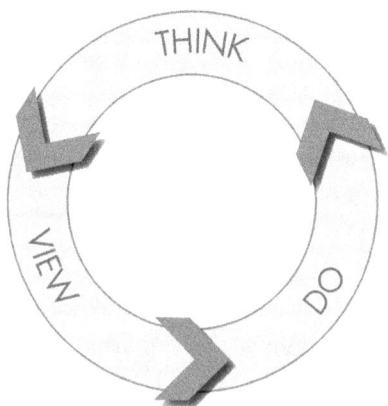

There's a certain way you're thinking, and your mind is leading you with an endless stream of thoughts—**THINK**. Your belief system, also known as your bias, is your perspective through which you see the world—**VIEW**. Your view you have of the world is based on your upbringing and directs you in a subconscious way. We can go through life without even realising the effect it has on us. This perspective then leads to what you say and your actions—**DO**. These actions then lead you back to the thoughts that arise and so the cycle continues.

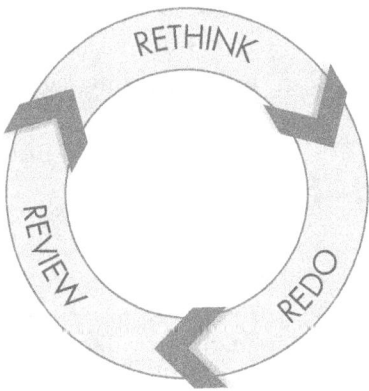

If we flip this cycle around, we can stop feeling stuck like a rat in a wheel, take ownership of our life, including our thoughts and environment. We learn about ourselves, we create awareness, we put it into action, and we create clarity. The cycle of unclogging is a three-step process:

1. RETHINK—understand who you are and what's at the core of you
2. REDO—implement what you know about yourself
3. REVIEW—reflect and continue committing to yourself

You become your own plumber. It's time to take care of your drain, your life. Know what keeps it flowing, maintain it so it doesn't clog up and if it does, go to your toolkit and use it to unclog.

WHAT IS UNCLOGGING?

> **Think about it as an audit cycle: continuously check yourself and continuously build your toolkit.**

It's an ongoing process, unclogging is a conscious one, becoming clogged is happening in a subconscious way. Think about it as an audit cycle: continuously check yourself and continuously build your toolkit. It's not going to be quick or easy, but we start aiming for simple. Also, be aware that the hardest part of the process is every time you start, but once you understand more of yourself it's going to become so much easier to implement. Stick with it, trust me and you'll be able to have the clarity you're longing for.

An unclogged life

Being able to go through life unclogged will gift you with clarity and control. Like an unclogged drain, things will be able to flow through, they don't have to affect you, and if they do, you will have the necessary tools to deal with them.

Going through the three steps in the next sections will set you on your way. And by continuously applying the steps of rethink, redo and review, the way you experience life and how you manage yourself and your surroundings will never be the same again. Here are some profound changes you can expect:

- You will be able to make decisions easier, quicker and better because you will learn to be prepared and armoured with self-knowledge that will provide you with the clarity of what you want and need.

- Your relationships will improve as you will be able to communicate with compassion and confidence because you will know what's important to you at any moment. But more important is that you willl be more present and less distracted as you have gained the skills to eliminate distractions.

- You will be calm because you will know how to constantly check in with yourself to assess your internal system, and how to adjust if something isn't right.

- You will be able to embrace change because you will learn that change is part of life. You will have a positive outlook that will allow you to see opportunities, not pitfalls.

- You will become more resilient and efficient as you will be using the tools that work for you and you will be prepared to adapt if the situation changes.

- You will be experiencing life as it should be; with joy and self-permission to truly be who you really are.

PART II
Rethink

This is the part of the process where you will:

Understand what makes you 'you'
and what the obstacles in your way are

Learn about what's going on in your mind

Be able to see things with positivity and purpose

Commit to understanding yourself

5

Know yourself

―

*"Very little is needed to make a happy life;
it is all within yourself, in your way of thinking."*
— Marcus Aurelius

Do you know the real you?

I'm going to tell you a big secret that's going to change your life. This is the single most important thing you can do for yourself: study yourself. I've always been a keen learner, but it took me 32 years to figure out that I also had to study myself. My dad used to say, "self-awareness is the beginning of wisdom" and my mum always said, "be true to yourself". Putting those things together now, combined with what've I learned, been taught and implemented, I know for sure that it is our duty to first and foremost understand ourselves. We can't fix the world or our partner for that matter, if we haven't had a hard look in the mirror at ourselves first.

If you really want to change your world, you first have to understand it.

KNOW YOURSELF

Self-study is one of the core principles of the ancient tradition of yoga. It's called in Sanskrit Svādhyāya and it's part of the first of the eight core building blocks of yoga. It's one of the virtues any traditionally schooled yogi lives by. And you don't have to become a yogi or even be interested in yoga to understand how essential self-study is. You can't wait for the world to give you what you need unless you yourself know what it is. Over time, by really reflecting on yourself you're steadily creating awareness, which is the starting point for all change.

Really, my life started changing as soon as I committed to my own studies. Remember that I committed to reading, I should say study, one book every month for a year? A non-fiction self-development book like this, whatever sparked my interest and whether I agreed with the content or not, I was going to learn something from it.

> You can't wait for the world to give you what you need unless you yourself know what it is.

I couldn't blame my work, or being busy, or any other excuse for not being able to learn, grow and develop myself. I needed to take matters in my own hands. And helpful for you; over the years I've studied somewhere between 50 to 100 of these books and I'm going to tell you exactly what you can do for yourself. Remember I'm efficient, without the fluff and very pragmatic. You might wonder how does one study yourself, where do you start, what do you need to do? Let's begin…

TIME TO UNCLOG

As you're starting out to find your own unique way to unclog, it would be helpful to identify what exactly isn't working well for you.

- **Let's start really easy**: Schedule about 15-20 minutes for yourself and write down right now what you'd mostly like to learn. What's not going well in your life? Try to get specific around the reason for picking this book. This will help you get even more out of this book as you've started with a clear motive of what you need.

How does this support unclogging?

It all starts with you. This is your life and you need to be able to manage it. Taking responsibility for what you know about yourself is the first step towards the unclogging of your life.

Your philosophy

To get to the core of you, first find out what's most important to you. Do you know what your values are? They make up your belief system, your philosophy. They make up you, what you strive for in life, what you hold dear. They are your driving forces.

It's vital to know clearly what your values are. When I ask my clients what their values are before we begin working together, they're usually valid albeit slightly non-specific values such as family, health, honesty or financial freedom. Completely understandable and reasonable, but what do they really mean? What does that give you? The more specific you get, the clearer your motives become what you're striving for and it can help to steer you in the right direction.

When you know your values, you can align your actions with them. Even your thoughts. Let me highlight this by the example of a conversation. I have a friend, his name is Ben. Ben is a new dad and like most dads, he was challenged by managing the situation around a young child. Now, exactly a year in, he had many first birthday parties to attend and he was getting a bit sick of them. But he anyway attended as his wife wanted him to accompany her, but with some resistance and he mentioned this to me. And this is how it could've worked out for him. If his most important values were family, support and love; he could go and alter his thoughts about the situation to an altruistic point of view that would allow him to fulfil those values. If he rates health, independence and passion very high; he then may be able to choose for himself, cancel attending a few of the upcoming celebrations and use that time to go for a run. You can align your actions with your beliefs, it's a simple choice you can make.

For me, getting clear on my values was the most important thing I have done for myself. It came with a sense of self-acceptance and a realisation of understanding why I do the things I do. But let's first get back to your values. On page 54, is the exercise I've advised all my clients to complete.

After you've completed the exercise, we'll get to how to utilise these values in the next part of the book when we move on to taking action. But for now, just focus on the interesting things that come up. Does it already highlight some aspects of your life? Perhaps you can see why certain things easily frustrate you (about yourself or others) or why you get so passionate about certain topics and now understand why others may not share that passion.

For me, this exercise was very insightful. It's interesting how we can go through life feeling unhappy, but we never dig a bit deeper to find out what our core beliefs are. Wouldn't it make more sense that that's where we should start? Well, I certainly think so.

Finding 20 to 30 values that resonated with me, which is the start of the exercise, was pretty straightforward and grouping them also wasn't that hard as I knew exactly what they meant to me, although I had to spend a bit of time on that. My challenge started around prioritising them. My two main grouped values were: neatness / tidiness / structure / clarity; and reflection / silence / calmness. My ideal self would've loved that I took more time for myself to sit down and read or meditate, but when I had a close look at what I actually do; I empty the dishwasher first and tidy up laundry before I start meditating. Annoying? Well, I thought so at first, but it wasn't until I realised that that's how I support myself. I could stay with the ideal and wishful version of myself and get frustrated that once again I didn't sit down reading this morning. Or I could accept the fact that this is more important to me in the real world, whether I like it or not. Realising that was almost a sense of release. I could let go of what I think I should be doing, and I could let go of all the other values that others or society holds dear and be okay with my own values. I didn't have to chase all the others anymore, or at least not as much, as they didn't mean that much to me. And that was totally okay.

A final note; these values can change over time. Usually, before we're in our fifties we tend to take health for granted, in our thirties we tend to focus on financial stability, and in our twenties, we're driven by fun and passion. This is, of course, a generalised view, but you understand that even though this list is the core of who you are, it's who you are right now. Don't tattoo them on your body as they will change. Usually not drastically, but it's important to be aware of that.

Don't identify yourself with them too much either. They are very strong indicators of how you operate but don't use them as an all fulfilling prophecy. One day, other aspects might be more important, and it can also be situational (weekend versus workdays). I'd say don't overcomplicate it and compile the list in the way it best resonates with you.

TIME TO UNCLOG

From the list of 180 values as listed on page 56 and 57, we will end up with a list of about 8-10 grouped values that represents your philosophy in life. To make it easier for you, you can download this worksheet on www.evebroenland.com/unclogging. Let's start.

- **Identify**: From this list, highlight the ones that resonate most with you and/or cross out the ones that absolutely don't. And you can be a bit ruthless here as all these values are probably good to have, but on a deeper level, they might not mean that much to you. It's not so much the focus on being aspirational here, but if you take some quiet time for yourself, you'll easily get the ones that mean the most to you. Don't overthink it, just start highlighting, underlining and crossing out. Keep going until you've narrowed it down to about 20 to 30 values. If you have more left, I know for sure you can eliminate more. You will find ones that won't stand out as much as the others. This is to gain your first deep insight into yourself, so no need to complicate this as the clearer you are the more it will help you in the long run.

- **Group**: Now you're going to group your 20 or so values in a way it makes sense to you. Are there a few that mean the same things to you? Are there a few that relate to each other? It's also very insightful to consider how you interpret this value. At one of my workshops, I had two ladies who both rated financial independence as one of their top values. However, their ethnicity had a huge effect on their interpretation. For the European woman, this meant freedom, self-reliance, and independence. But for the woman from an Asian background, it was linked to family, stability, and care. To group them really strengthens their meaning. It clarifies on a deeper level what they mean to you.

- **Prioritise**: You now have about 8-10 groups of values that strongly resonate with you, let's put them in the right order. When prioritising them we get clear on what beliefs are most important to you, but we have to make a clear distinction here; your ideal self vs your real self. Yes, perhaps in an ideal world we all would put caring and compassion first, but if you're most driven by wealth and your willingness to succeed, then that's okay. Forget what the world wants, forget what your friends and family want, this is about you. There is no judgement because if you do judge, the list is not going to be a full representation of what you believe in. How can you best prioritise? Think about what you actually do on a daily basis. Let's say you have fitness/health/self-care as one grouped values and wealth/financial independence/stability as another. Do you wake up early to exercise? Then probably the health will be put first. But if you work long hours and cut down on sleep sometimes to get that proposal finished, then probably the second one should be put first. Only you know the right answer, no one else can give it to you.

Values

Abundance	Commitment	Discretion
Acceptance	Community	Diversity
Accomplishment	Compassion	Drive
Accountability	Competition	Ease
Achievement	Confidence	Education
Acknowledgement	Congruency	Effectiveness
Adaptability	Conservation	Efficiency
Adventure	Consistency	Elegance
Affection	Contentment	Empathy
Affluence	Continuity	Energy
Alertness	Contribution	Enjoyment
Ambition	Control	Entertainment
Appreciation	Cooperation	Enthusiasm
Assertiveness	Correctness	Environmentalism
Balance	Courage	Excitement
Beauty	Creativity	Experience
Belonging	Credibility	Expertise
Calmness	Curiosity	Fairness
Capability	Daring	Faith
Certainty	Decisiveness	Family
Challenge	Dependability	Financial independence
Change	Desire	Fitness
Clarity	Determination	Flexibility
Cleanliness	Diligence	Focus
Comfort	Discipline	Freedom

Friendship	Mindfulness	Satisfaction
Fun	Modesty	Security
Generosity	Motivation	Self-reliance
Gratitude	Nature	Selflessness
Growth	Open-mindedness	Sensuality
Health	Openness	Serenity
Helpfulness	Optimism	Sexuality
Honesty	Organization	Sharing
Humility	Outdoors	Significance
Humor	Partnership	Simplicity
Hygiene	Passion	Sincerity
Imagination	Patience	Skillfulness
Independence	Peace	Solidarity
Influence	Perceptiveness	Solitude
Ingenuity	Perfection	Spirituality
Inquisitiveness	Persistence	Spontaneity
Inspiration	Persuasiveness	Stability
Integrity	Pleasure	Stillness
Intelligence	Power	Strength
Intimacy	Pragmatism	Success
Intuition	Pride	Support
Inventiveness	Privacy	Sympathy
Joy	Professionalism	Teaching
Justice	Prosperity	Teamwork
Keenness	Rationality	Thankfulness
Kindness	Realism	Trust
Knowledge	Recognition	Trustworthiness
Leadership	Reflection	Uniqueness
Learning	Relaxation	Usefulness
Liveliness	Religiousness	Variety
Logic	Resilience	Vision
Love	Respect	Vitality
Loyalty	Responsibility	Volunteering
Making a difference	Restraint	Wealth
Marriage	Sacredness	Zeal

- **Accept**: Have a good look at your list now. Is it you? What do you feel when you look at this list? Maybe you need to sit and evaluate it for a bit and make some minor adjustments, which is totally fine. This is your list and as you grow, your values can shift slightly too. It's always a good thing to reassess this list anyway. I'd give it a nice title such as *My Beliefs* or *My Philosophy* or *What Drives Me* or *What I Live By*. This is you. Isn't it amazing? Accept what your list is, there's no need to compare or feel bad that wealth is number one on your list. There's absolutely no judgement here. This is what you live by, this is the core of who you are right now. And it's beautifully unique to you. I can guarantee you there is no one else who has these values grouped and prioritised the way you have. Cherish this, and well done on taking this first step.

- **Learn**: Finally make sure you know your values, don't file them away and forget about them. I'd say print the list out and stick it on your fridge, or for the next few weeks make it the lock screen on your phone. This list is much too important not to have it close by. Have the values ingrained in your mind, so you can always refer to them. At least know your top 2 by heart. I promise you it'll make your life so much easier.

How does this support unclogging?

This is the first part of unclogging. Unclogging is letting go of what isn't the real you, based on your philosophy; the values you believe in. It eliminates so many of the struggles if we understand what's most important to us.

Your strengths

The next step is identifying what you're good at, the core of who you are and how you can succeed living in line with your values. You are given a unique set of talents and it's your responsibility to know them and develop them. What comes naturally to you doesn't come naturally to others. We sometimes like to think others operate in the same way we do, but they really don't.

You may have heard of the Myer-Briggs profile test to determine whether you work from intellect or intuition or you are more of an introvert or an extrovert, or the DISC behavioural profile test which determines if you are dominant, an influencer, a stable factor or if you're conscientious, a mix of two. These tests are extremely valuable for a more generic insight and are evidence that we're all different. We've already figured out that our values are unique, and the same accounts for our strengths.

> So much energy is wasted by us trying to build up what we're naturally not good at.

Why is it important to know your strengths? Remember we've talked about the tendency of us humans to fix what's not working and then adding more pressure onto ourselves? Donald Clifton describes in his wonderful book, first published 25 years ago and still very relevant, *Soar With Your Strengths* that we as a society tend to focus on our weaknesses. If a child comes home with a really good school rapport card, but there's one score slightly below average, that's the one we'll focus on. We will personally mentor, find a tutor, request extra homework; only to ensure the score will improve. But what if we instead focus on our strengths and develop them into our superpowers. Our strengths are the things that come naturally to us, which makes it even easier for us to develop them. So much energy is wasted by us trying to build up what we're naturally not good at. To me, it doesn't make sense. Focusing on your strengths makes things so much simpler.

In his book *The Big Leap*, Gay Hendricks talks about finding your zone of genius. He describes this zone as one where you're doing your best work, you excel, and you love what you're doing. By knowing what you're good at and utilising it to its full potential, you'll create the best possible environment for yourself.

Once you have identified your strengths (see page 62 and 63 for the exercise) and as per the values, label it appropriately and don't just file it away. Go back to your list, study your strengths, adjust if needed and reflect on how you're currently using them. Perhaps you're not fully utilising your strengths, or you're in an environment that doesn't contribute to you fulfilling your strengths. But that's no excuse, it's up to you to build on them. You can do that outside of work, start a project that excites you, or start learning something new relating to your talents. Never be afraid to soar. There's no point in playing down your strengths, the world needs you to use them. Believe in yourself. They're your gifts, own them, and it's up to you to develop them.

Although focussing on what you're great at is key to make your life simpler, you can't fully negate your weaknesses. We will always end up in situations, and for some unfortunately quite regularly, where we have to do things that don't work for us. There're a few things you can consider doing in such case:

1. **Eliminate**: Determine if you can eliminate the specific task, is it really necessary?
2. **Delegate**: Pass on your task to someone else. If you want to work optimally, you have to let go of certain tasks that don't work well for you.
3. **Collaborate**: Find someone who has a natural talent for these activities and utilise their awesomeness in collaboration with yours.
4. **Substitute**: Can you do something different? Instead of writing emails, can you send voice messages instead? Technology has been super helpful in substituting tasks.

5. **Adjust**: Can you alter the task in a way that works for you? It might be breaking up the task in sections or doing them in a different way that works better for you. Schedule that face to face meeting if you don't like making phone calls.

What is one of your challenges but still part of your daily life? For some, it's doing administration or the aspect of sales. As example, for me, it's writing this book. It's exceedingly challenging for me; I'm easily distracted, a multitude of thoughts occupy my mind and I love working with people. Here are my five options considering the above list:

1. Option 1 — I could quit the idea of writing this book, but that's doing you as the reader a disservice and doesn't align with how I want to share my message.
2. Option 2 — I could find a ghost writer, which was tempting, but I find it more important that this message comes directly from me.
3. Option 3 — In a way, I'm collaborating with people as I've got a wonderful group of peers holding me accountable and providing me with valuable feedback.
4. Option 4 — Instead of a book I could do videos or podcasts, and I will do them, but more in support of this book. And I think it's tremendously valuable for people being able to learn from reading.
5. Option 5 — What did I opt to do? I adjusted my task; I'm breaking it up in sections, in a structured way, so I'm not writing an entire book, but chapters which makes my writing much more manageable. And I've removed myself from other distractions and sitting by myself with a timeline makes a huge difference. While writing, I'm keeping you as the reader at the forefront of my mind, which in a way can be viewed as you and me having a very long conversation, which helps me tremendously with the writing of this book.

TIME TO UNCLOG

What are you good at? Let's find out what makes you unique and what talents you have that come naturally to you.

- **Figure out what your strengths are**: Here are a few options you have.

    o Take the Gallup Strengths Finder test. It's extremely insightful and it only takes about 30 to 40 minutes to complete. Having the same top five strengths as any other person is a chance of one in 33 million. Talking about unique. My top five strengths are: Activator, Input, Individualisation, Learner, Command and I purposefully aim to use them every day.

    o Write down for yourself what you're good at. Think about what you love doing, what you excel in, or what you're a quick learner in. These are all indicators helping you determine what your strengths are.

    o Another common, but in my opinion, a less favourable option, is asking people in your network to list three of your qualities. You can ask your boss or colleagues, your parents, your friends or people in your community. However, my reservation regarding this option is that it's the representation of what you put out there by getting results filtered through other people. Not entirely reliable, but if you're really stuck, this can be a good starting point.

o Think about your allergies; qualities of people that get under your skin or frustrate you immensely. These are usually linked with your strengths. The core quality quadrant, as depicted below, will help you get there, as your allergy is the opposite of your strength.

- **Build your strengths**: Set yourself three goals of how you can start building on your strengths on a daily basis. Find tasks that align with your strengths, such as reading 10 minutes every day if you have a passion for learning.

How does this support unclogging?

We waste so much of our energy and motivation while working outside our zone of genius. It makes everything in life much simpler to hone in on your natural talents and skills. Let go of your weaknesses, build on your strengths and everything will be less challenging and overwhelming.

Your body

Knowing your body is an imperative aspect of knowing yourself. It's not only the purely physical aspect of your body but also how your body responds to its external influences. Being able to read your body will help you understand yourself and break some of your habits or automatic responses. And we can use it to our advantage to manage and even manipulate our internal system.

As a yoga and martial arts practitioner, I know how important it is to be in tune with your body. The physical supports the emotional and spiritual. My personal challenge is always my shoulders. Most of the time I have very tense shoulders and neck muscles, and you don't have to dig far to notice a big tight knot in there. It's my weak spot and will often cause me discomfort. Only up until a few years ago, did I notice I tense my shoulders by default. I pull them up towards my ears, and it's causing a huge tension in my neck, but it's also extremely exhausting. And when I say default mode; I do this when I chop vegetables, sit on the sofa to relax or talking on the phone. I think it's even happened during my morning walk with the dogs. It's really totally unnecessary to be that tense, but it clearly is something that's become a habit of mine. However, as soon as I realised this, I could use that awareness to let go of the tension. It doesn't happen overnight, and it's still work in progress, but for me to intently relax has definitely helped me. And it becomes clear when I experience tension when I get stressed or triggered, so it's an obvious sign for me.

In her famous book, sold over 35 million times, *You Can Heal Your Life* the late Louise Hay described how your mind influences your body, but also how you can use your illnesses as an indication of what's really troubling you. Her key message, that you can heal any illness by doing the inner work, might be a bit controversial, but I recognise the interconnection between the two. While struggling and feeling stressed, you might also get headaches easily or you're always the one to catch a cold first. I'm no expert in healing your body, so I'm only pointing this out because of the fact that you can use any physical challenges as indicators that you are clogged. The more awareness you have, the quicker you can do something about it.

Another body expert, Amy Cuddy in her famous TED talk describes how we can use our body to manipulate how we feel. For instance, using a strong stance for two minutes, like hands on your hips and your legs shoulder width apart, induces long lasting hormone release and make you feel more confident. It has a huge effect on your own emotional system and to how others perceive us, all through the use of your body language. And the first rule of the twelve life rules in *12 Rules for Life* is to have your shoulders pulled back (something very valuable I've learned). Jordan Peterson describes in depth that lobsters in a fight for dominance don't necessarily fight, they just have to exude dominance. And it's not the larger individual that wins. If he won the previous fight the lobster gains confidence and will most likely conquer again.

Being able to check in with your body and becoming aware of the signs of stress or tension, helps you acting more pro-active. Stress signs are very clear indicators and it's such a simple way to learn more about yourself.

TIME TO UNCLOG

Here are a few things you can start with to understand your body better, build that relationship and have your body cooperate with your mind and environment in a way that suits you best.

- **Learn to breathe**: Take deep and mindful breaths whenever you can but especially when you're stressed. Many books have been written on this topic and eastern philosophies acknowledge how essential conscious breathing is. The reason for it being so powerful and effective is it being the only bodily process from the parasympathetic nervous system you can control. You can't control your digestion or the contractions of your heart, but you can control your breathing. And it's a fact that by taking deep and slow breaths your stress hormones lower and you'll feel calmer and experience a sense of bliss.

- **Observe and relax**: When in a stressful situation observe how your body is responding. Are your shoulders hunched? Is your jaw tight? Or do you have your toes curled? Start paying attention to these cues as you'll learn a lot from yourself that way and relax whenever you can. Stretch and relax.

- **Connect with your body**: Establish a relationship with your body. Yoga is a fantastic way to connect with your body, but I also get the same benefits from my martial arts training or even running. Moving with intention and mindfully, and letting go of your fitness objectives or expectations of what your body should be doing, will enable you checking in what you're feeling and doing on a much deeper level. Just stay in the moment.

- **Appreciate and take care of your body:** You only have one body so you might as well start loving it and it's your duty to take care of. Let it work to your advantage, in the present and in the future. Perhaps exercise a bit more, eat healthier, as ultimately how you treat your body is directly related to how your mind is operating. If you want to feel less overwhelmed, you have to work for it. But do what works for you.

How does this support unclogging?

Your body is such a powerful indicator of how you're doing on the inside. By creating awareness and learning how to relax, your entire system will become so much more capable, attuned to and open to unclogging.

KNOW YOURSELF

Goals

It's human nature to set goals and most of us do have goals, but the way we venture into it, is completely different. Some people write down their goals and go through a diligent goal setting process every year and do a reassessment every three to six months. Most of us probably have goals in the back of our heads and it's something we're working towards without a set deadline. Some people declare their goals to their friends or on social media to help them feel more inspired and keeping them accountable. There are many ways of taking on goals and I'll be outlining the different approaches below. Most important at this stage of the rethinking process, is uncovering the reason behind these goals. Are you clear on the reason for you chasing this goal and is it really what you want?

For me going through this process, I realised my ambition being a marine biologist and climbing the corporate ladder, wasn't really me. And accepting this wasn't an easy process as it was something I believed in since my early teens. But thinking back now, when you're 14, you've got an idea in your head what this career would look like and what it would do for you. Of course, that's not how it will actually pan out and it also may not correspond with who you are (which I'm still trying to figure out now, let alone knowing that at the age of 14). It seems only logical to reassess those goals and giving yourself permission letting go of them if they're no longer what you want. Our society applauds persistence, and there's absolute value in this virtue, but only to a certain extent. If you're doing things only for the sake of your earlier commitment to it, I'd say it's time to reassess.

What are the best ways of setting goals? There are many approaches and you have to do what suits you best. Are you a planner or a doer? As a doer, I might want to suggest you spend a bit of extra time on the goal setting area as even though it doesn't come naturally to you, it'll be worth your while so you don't waste time on moving in the wrong direction. And as a planner myself, I need to be very careful not to go in over-planning mode, just a few clear goals will support me going forward, but getting bogged down in all minuscule details definitely doesn't. So, let's find out what works for you.

Goal setting approach

Using SMART goals is the most common goal setting approach available and it's a beautiful acronym that helps you clarifying the details and enabling you to measure your success.

Specific — what in particular are you going to achieve?
Measurable — provide a way to evaluate how you'll achieve it.
Achievable — ensure it is possible for you to achieve it.
Relevant — does it make sense for you to achieve it?
Timely — set a clear timeframe for you to achieve it.

I love the clarity of this approach, but it can also be quite rigid. For a business environment, like a Key Performance Indicator setting for your annual targets, using this approach makes a lot of sense. It's clear to both parties and progress can be clearly tracked. However, for your purpose of what you want out of life, I wouldn't suggest this approach. It's quite rigid and may not excite you much.

In his book *Flow*, Mihaly Csikszentmihalyi, one of the founding positive psychologists, describes the most optimal state of conscious satisfaction. In this state, we're completely absorbed in an activity, especially an activity that involves using our talents and creativity. Csikszentmihalyi outlines that clarity of goals is paramount, it's the first condition of achieving this state of flow, 'being in the zone'. He describes the difference between outcome goals and process goals. Outcome goals are your long-term vision, what you're working towards, but process goals are the small targets you set to get you there. Differentiating the two will ensure you can align your actions with your vision. Gaining clarity on your goals will support you in getting to your optimum mode of operating.

Lastly, I'd like to highlight the fantastic work of Danielle LaPorte. In her book *The Desire Map*, she stresses the importance of our emotions within our goal setting. Her heart-based approach ensures you are emotionally connected to your goal, which will be the key motivator for you taking action. Does it inspire and excite you? And how will it make you feel? Asking yourself these questions will shed an entirely different light on your goals and will further clarify your motivators. At the end of the day, isn't how we feel more important than what we've accomplished?

A final note: don't view goals as rigid actions you are obliged achieving as this will once again put pressure on you. The key is to clarify what excites you and what will inspire you towards taking action. It's all about the vision you have for yourself and what makes you feel good. And whenever necessary, give yourself permission to reassess and adjust. This is your life and you can take any direction you choose to go, it's just simpler when you know which direction to take.

> *"Let go of your goals, so they can find you."*
> *— ROGER HAMILTON*

TIME TO UNCLOG

Let's reassess where you'd like to go, what your aim is, what's truly important to you, in this very moment. Reassessment is valuable as you may still be holding on to goals that no longer serve you, but you can now redefine new ones ensuring you feel excited about making changes in your life.

- **Choose an area**: It's sometimes helpful to first compartmentalise areas of your life. What is your biggest challenge right now? Your health, career, relationships or maybe your finances? Pick one or two areas you're most keen to see working better for you.

- **Identify what you want**: Write down what you want more of in this area of your life and perhaps you'd like adding a few time frame indicators like three months, six months, one year, or three years to help you see the bigger picture. Don't overthink or filter too much here, it's much easier writing down everything that comes up, and simplifying it later on.

- **Know why**: For each goal ask yourself the reason for you wanting to achieve this goal. What would it do for you if you've achieved it? If you can't mention a reason, it's probably not what you're really after. You need to know the purpose before you can go after it.

- **Know what**: For each goal write down the specifics. What would it present you with? What changes have taken place and what are the effects? What does it look like? The last question may seem like overkill, however going visual really helps you to further refine your goal. Plus, it'll be one of the most powerful tools for you towards the achievement of your goals.

- **Read your list**: Now that you have your goals clearly defined, I want you to read them out loud. When you read them, they need to invoke a positive emotion. Does it excite you? What feelings do you experience? Write this down underneath the goal too. To lose 10 kg is merely an action; to get fit is purposeful, but to feel confident and sexy is life changing.

- **One final check**: Do the goals really belong to you? Check the possibility of this goal being subconsciously set by yourself. Were they not set by someone else, society or by your previous self? It will be very difficult to answer this with certainty, but it's helpful taking a moment reviewing this. Is losing the 10 kg important to you or to society? Although sometimes hard to differentiate, it's worth taking into consideration.

How does this support unclogging?

Being clear on your goals carves the way for you directing your energy towards what matters most to you. You'll be able to clearly identify if outside influences are supportive or distractive. And this will make the difference between being clogged or unclogged.

Key points

- Continuously study yourself — commit to 30 minutes of learning every day.
- Get clear on your values.
- Stop focussing on your weaknesses and start owning your strengths.
- Tune into your body more and take a few deep breaths during the day to relax and connect with yourself.
- Let go of goals that don't serve you anymore.

Implementation

Develop a personal mission statement that outlines:

- Your beliefs and what strive for in life.
- Your strengths and how you will use them.
- Your goals and why you want to achieve them.

Further learning

- Soar with Your Strengths - Donald Clifton
- The Desire Map - Danielle LaPorte
- Flow - Mihaly Csikszentmihalyi
- Yoga Mind, Body & Spirit - Donna Farhi
- The Big Leap - Gay Hendricks
- Heal Your Life - Louise Hay

6

Adding positivity

―――

*"I know of no more encouraging fact than
the unquestionable ability of man to elevate
his life by a conscious endeavour."*
— Thoreau

Assumptions & perceptions

Now that you've taken the first step and know more of who you are and what's really important to you, I'd like to delve a bit further into you and another key aspect of the rethinking phase. Rethinking starts with an understanding of yourself, but most definitely also how you think and perceive the world.

People used to think we'd fall off the earth if we travelled too far. The correction of a simple, yet false assumption moved the human race forward. You can do the same for yourself. We all have a lens through which we see the world. This perception is based on what you've learned, what you believe, the experiences you had and also the stories you built up around that background. The stories we create stems from us never

> **The correction of a simple, yet false assumption moved the human race forward. You can do the same for yourself.**

being able to fully take in our environment and then ending up automatically creating assumptions. The way we've learned to take in our environment is helpful, otherwise, we would've become exhausted from all the inputs. However, when it comes to learned beliefs (assumptions we make or have learned from our parents) they can be limiting us. Those beliefs run your mind and therefore determine how you perceive your world. As Bruce Lipton states in the *Biology of Belief*: *"the function of the mind is to create coherence between our beliefs and the reality we experience."* It's now your bias, and unfortunately, subconsciously it has a tremendous and potentially limiting effect on you. Barry Neil Kaufman, in his book *Son Rise*, adds to this with his wisdom: *"the way we choose to see the world, creates the world we see"*.

There is hence lots of merit in ensuring your perception of the world is one that is supportive of you. If you believe the world is a bad place and it's always going to be a struggle, well then, it's most definitely going to stay that way. We need to be aware of the assumptions we have and make.

Overcome negativity bias

We fear the unknown and we're wired to see the negative in our world. This is how our body and mind system operate; it would rather stay safe and in the familiar and known than the unfamiliar and unknown. This uncertainty causes your brain to write its own story which is a.) not accurate and b.) usually negative.

This is how it works in the brain; the amygdala serves as the emotional switchboard, receiving information from the senses and then signalling the rest of the brain and nervous system ways to respond. One of the responses is detecting new or threatening elements in the environment that result in the freeze, fight or flight response.

From an evolutionary perspective, this entirely makes sense; this is what kept us alive as we evolved from living in small groups of hunters and gatherers. Our brain is designed to react swiftly to danger, it'll do so instinctively. Our ears perk up when we hear gossip, when the phone rings at unusual times we automatically imagine the worst and that's the main reason for bad and dramatic news selling so well. The media uses this to their advantage. But have you ever wondered how it affects you? These instinctive behaviours absolutely served (and to a point still serve) a purpose, but we do live in a completely different environment. And the development of our brains is not evolving at the same rate as our changing society.

Mindset is everything

Have you ever watched the reality series Alone? In this show they select ten survival experts to go out into the wilderness with a limited amount of supplies, all in different locations and they have to survive. It's as tough and real as it can get; shelter, fire, food, and water all need to be taken care of by the participants. At their own discretion, they can use their satellite phone to leave the wilderness. The person who sticks it out in the wilderness the longest wins the cash prize. I love watching this show as you can almost guess who the winner is going to be based on the mindsets they have. Did their camp get wet? Did the gill net break? Do they constantly see this as setbacks to make adjustments or redo some work, or do they see it as constant challenges they need to overcome?

Research has revealed when in a negative mindset, everything feels more challenging and heavier, even impossible, we give up more easily or we don't even try (Shawn Achor - *Before Happiness*). The psychological state of mind of participants in this show has a huge effect on their success and the duration of their survival stay: they see possibilities and opportunities, their energy levels are higher and they enjoy the experience more. One participant even referred to it as 'wilderness living' instead of surviving. Isn't that a great way of looking at it?

I'd like to explain this further through the work that's been done in the field of positive psychology. Positive psychologists have proven you can change your mindset, retrain your brain and therefore change your life. This is really rethinking.

Of all the actions we take, only 5% are on a conscious level. The rest is habitual, subconsciously, and goes unnoticed to us. This subconscious part, which involves the majority of the way you go through life, is steered by what you believe of yourself and your environment (as described in the previous section) and results in the actions you take (which we'll get to in Part III). Most of the time we run on autopilot. Our neurological pathways are wired by the age of 30-35 years, our personalities are then fully developed, and we have accustomed ourselves to our environment. However, if your assumptions are negatively skewed or not serving your personal growth, it will limit you in making changes. It has to start in your mind, with the belief that it's possible and doable. It's therefore essential to become aware of the subconscious side of yourself, your autopilot and your beliefs.

To stop negativity from unnecessarily affecting you, but also protecting you from the potential of your thoughts overdramatising situations, it's important to utilise your logic and objective outlook. As the late Hans Rosling puts so well in his book *Factfulness*: *"Factfulness, like a healthy diet and regular exercise, can and should become part of your daily life. You will make better decisions, stay alert to real dangers, and avoid being constantly stressed about the wrong things."*

It's so important to gain an understanding of your thoughts as they can literally rule your life. We spend a lot of time in our heads, especially with everything going on in our lives. Aim to be objective and on occasion challenge your thoughts; you now know they don't have to be true and that they tend to go in a negative direction. And this, of course, can really affect you.

TIME TO UNCLOG

This is not a quick fix activity, I'm giving you a few starting points to raise your awareness. The rethinking part of the unclogging process is a continuous exploration of yourself, and this is definitely one of them. Here's what you can do:

- **Become aware of habits**: Things you're doing automatically, you're taking for granted or stating as a fact about yourself, especially if using the word 'always' in such a statement. Or go and do something you normally wouldn't do and question yourself why that is. Give yourself some space to explore your habits.

- **Look at it from a different perspective**: If training yourself through the following simple technique, you can start retaining your brain. It also helps you to get out of a fixed mindset mode. When you're in a certain situation, let's say someone does something you wouldn't do, and you don't understand their action. Your mind will automatically fill in the reason why the other person did what he/she did (remember, we don't like uncertainty). However, this assumption cannot be interpreted as a fact. Come up with three different scenarios, rather than just the one, for the reason why this person acted that way. They might be completely wrong scenarios, but it'll help you view it from another perspective.

- **Create a favourable mindset**: Before undertaking something challenging, such as making a phone call to an unknown person or asking your boss for a favour, take a moment getting into the best mindset. What do you need to say to yourself before making that call? Perhaps it might be reminding yourself why you're wanting to do this, or that you'll be proud of yourself for taking that step. List all the positives, no matter what the outcome and support yourself that way.

How does this support unclogging?

Becoming aware of your subconscious behaviour will uncover your reasons why certain elements of your life feel like a challenge. Getting clogged through set behavioural patterns happens easily as you don't even realise it's happening. By challenging your own assumptions and actively aiming to change your mindset and perspective will help you unclog.

Happiness

Happiness is such a hot topic these days. It's almost being used as frequently as mindfulness. But what is happiness? More importantly though, do you know what happiness means to you? Of course, here we need to distance ourselves from short-term pleasure-seeking activities but agree that we're referring to long-lasting feelings of joy.

A considerable amount of research is being done in the field of happiness as we're all curious to find out what gives us that feeling. Our standard of living has grown exponentially, yet we know that this hasn't made us any happier. Beside the GDP Index, countries are also being assessed based on their satisfaction level through the Global Happiness Index. The majority of the Scandinavian countries, and The Netherlands, are holding the top spots. I find it fascinating how our society is evolving this way. It's great that we look at more than just economic growth to observe the world we live in. It's almost similar to transitioning from using not just your intellect, but also incorporating your emotions.

But what is happiness? Dr. Martin Seligman, Director of the *Center of Authentic Happiness* and author of the same titled book formulates happiness as follows:

$$H = S + C + V$$

Which indicates that:
- H - Your lasting level of happiness is equal to the sum of
- S - Your set range; the limits of your happiness through barriers of your beliefs. (This is the reason why most people winning the Lotto don't end up happier, as their set range will bring them down again.)
- C - Your circumstance; the environment you live in.
- V - Factors under your voluntary control; the things you can change.

Even though S and C are difficult to change, the opportunities lie in V.

This realistic and pragmatic representation of happiness outlines that it lies within your power to change your level of happiness. The following section is how to apply that to you personally, and Chapter 10 is focused on how to work on factor V through your interactions with others.

This is my favourite quote on happiness;

> *"Maybe happiness is this: not feeling that you should be elsewhere, doing something else, being someone else."*
> – ERIC WEINER

For me, happiness is being content and in the moment. Not comparing the situation to anything else, not complaining, or wishing things to be different. Don't make it conditional. Feel gratitude and joy without needing a person, thing or experience to cause you to feel that way. The key is becoming independent of external cues. That's what I'm aiming for in life.

Gratitude

Gratitude is the simplest way to choose happiness every day. When you feel sincerely grateful, other negative feelings can't exist. All negative feelings dissipate when one is truly grateful. Appreciate and focus on the good events and focus less on the bad ones.

While you're still retraining your brain into a more positive approach, the simplest exercise is coming up with three new things you're grateful for. Shawn Achor describes this proven technique in his successful book *Before Happiness* and his TED talk. By coming up with three new things every day, you're teaching your brain to be on the lookout for positivity. It's literally rewiring your neurological pathways. Over time you'll experience more joy and have a higher level of long-term happiness, only because you've learned to look at the positives. So simple, but super effective.

TIME TO UNCLOG

Have you ever wondered what happiness means to you? If you're clear on what it is for you, you'll be able to build on it too.

- **What is happiness for you?** Take some time to answer this question. What does it mean for you? Is it being calm and content? Is it making a difference? Is it spiritual? Or is it taking care of loved ones? Most likely it's linked to your values.

- **What limits you from being happy?** Being able to answer this question will help you, as it can significantly increase your awareness. You'll be able to use this answer as an indicator for getting clogged (more on that later). For me, it used to be comparing myself to others. And the minute I caught myself scrolling mindlessly on Facebook, I knew straight away this was not supporting me.

- **Practice gratitude**: Write down three new things you're grateful for each day. Do this for at least 21 days straight and check in with yourself to see how it has changed your perspective.

How does this support unclogging?

Actively working towards increasing your level of long-term happiness will make your life feel easier. This calmness will automatically reduce the number of disturbances you have as you will pay less attention to them and your chances of getting clogged will be less likely.

Emotional clarity

> *"Happiness belongs to those who are in control of their circumstances and their emotions."*
> – Jim Rohn

We choose our emotions based on our perceptions. In the first section of this chapter, we discussed our assumptions and perceptions and unfortunately, they also affect how we choose our emotions.

Let's take the following example: You're driving in your car on your way to work and a person in front of you is driving about 10km/h below the speed limit. You're in a hurry and you're getting annoyed. You're now right behind the car and you have to brake. You notice the driver is a man. "*What's wrong with you*" and "*geez, just hurry up*" are thoughts going through your mind. You're now really getting impatient and you hit the horn. Still no change, and now you're really feeling agitated and you become frustrated as you realise you won't have time for a coffee before your first meeting of the day. Then onwards, approaching an intersection, the man causes an accident. Your first response is that of shock that the man is such a bad driver and you shake your head in disbelief. At the same time, you become a bit alarmed and worried. Is he okay? A person from the sidewalk already approached the man's car and you park your car to see if you can help. Apparently, the man is having a heart attack. He probably wasn't feeling well and that was the reason for him driving so slowly. You instantly feel guilty. As you walk over to the car, you notice it's your dad and your heart sinks into your boots.

Nothing in the story changed except your perception. You created your own reality around it, and you chose to feel annoyed, frustrated, disbelief, worried, guilty and finally despair. If you were able to look at it from another perspective, you would've been able to control your emotions. You don't have to get frustrated, that's a choice you're making. Building on your emotional clarity is challenging and probably a lifelong journey, but starting with the less intense emotions, such as annoyance, irritability, and impatience, will be a great starting point.

Emotions also influence your rational mind and have a large effect on your decision-making ability. If the emotion is still present, it will cloud your judgement and affect the choices you make. The story could've also ended with you getting a speed ticket or causing an accident yourself as your frustrations caused you to speed. It's essential for your wellbeing to know you can choose a different emotion and to do so will absolutely have a positive effect on you.

Choose positivity

I've always been a positive person, but more eminent is my continual belief (and now I also know) that we can choose positivity. We can decide to be happy, to be content, or to experience joy. Being able to grow this skill and putting it into practice has made many situations in my life so much easier. Several years ago, when I got made redundant from my job as an environmental professional, the initial processing of the notification that I've lost my job lasted about 30 minutes. But I instantly knew this was going to be the best thing that has ever happened to me. I didn't fret over the smaller or bigger details; I didn't blame anyone or became resentful. I was going to tackle this head on and work it out. And because of that, I'm now able to do what I'm good at, what I love and making a difference in people's lives. As Mary Poppins (my absolute favourite movie of all times) used to say: *"a spoon full of sugar helps the medicine go down"*.

Just sprinkle a dose of positivity on top. That is what positive psychologists refer to as learned optimism. Shawn Achor in his fantastic book *Before Happiness* refers to: use your brain as a pair of Bose noise cancelling headphones. There are two ways to block out noise (negativity), one is passive, which means putting in earplugs and blocking the noise. The active way is through noise cancelling headphones; they actively emit opposite sound waves to cancel out the noise. For any negativity, we thus need to work towards actively seeking out positivity.

If you're still new at this, below are two main aspects to keep in mind and they go hand in hand. And this is how you can apply them:

1. **Be aware of a negative attitude**: This is most of the time a habitual response to something that you've developed a dislike for over time. But be especially mindful when perceiving it as being permanent or universal. The keywords here are 'always', 'never', 'all' and 'are'. Be very careful of generalising statements as over time they will become ingrained in you.
2. **Seek other positive perspectives**: Seek evidence that the negative viewpoint is false. Remember that our brains quickly try processing our surroundings and are inclined to make incorrect and negative assumptions. Best is finding a way to overcome this by coming up with three scenarios of interpretations. (As per one of the actions suggested in the previous paragraph.)

> *"Happiness is not about being blind to the negatives in our environment, but it's about believing we have the power to do something about it."*
> – Shawn Achor

Researcher Kazuo Murakami even hypothesises that through positive thinking certain genes can be switched on or off, thereby resulting in a more beneficial outcome. In his book *The Divine Code of Life*, he refers to this process as 'genetic thinking'. This could explain why a happy smoker may never develop lung cancer or an in-love student suddenly excels in his studies. Research in this field is still expanding, however not fully conclusive at this stage.

Plentiful research is conducted in the field of how our minds work and how our minds steer us. I love learning more about it as it has such a huge impact on how we perceive the world and live our lives. Even though what is outlined in this chapter is only a snippet of the knowledge out there, you hopefully now understand it's important to you and the quality of your life to become aware of your thoughts and emotions. It's in your power to add more positivity to your life.

TIME TO UNCLOG

There are some simple ways to consciously bring more positivity in your life. It's just up to you to decide to implement them. Try them, but perhaps, more importantly, is to remind yourself of them during the day.

- **Smile**: Everything is perceived with more positivity when you have a smile on your face. You even breathe better and even if you fake the smile, it will trick your system and bring about a positive effect.

- **Decide differently**: The next time your morning commute isn't going the way you planned; you missed the bus or traffic is really bad, decide there and then that it's not going to affect you. This is challenging as your habitual self will want to vent and fume, but you don't have to get annoyed at all.

- **Don't feed the negative emotions**: When they emerge, just let the emotion dissipate. If you try to fight it, it will expand. Let it be and when it's not overwhelming, choose a more positive attitude instead.

- **Say thank you to the unexpected or the negative**: Be grateful for the bills coming in as that means you're in the fortunate position of being able to afford them. If you can approach any difficulty coming your way with a different approach, your outlook on life will change forever.

How does this support unclogging?

Having emotional clarity will ensure when life gets challenging and you might get clogged, you'll be able to deal with the disruptions with much more ease.

Key points

- Become aware of false assumptions providing you with a negative view of your surroundings.
- Know what happiness is and what it means to you.
- You can choose positive thoughts and emotions.

Implementation

Rewire your brain so your world can become more positive:

- Take time to reflect on what happiness is to you. It's probably closely linked to your values.
- Work on raising your awareness to eliminate negative subconscious behaviour.
- Practice gratitude.

Further learning

- Authentic Happiness - Martin Seligman
- Before Happiness - Shawn Achor
- Happiness and How It Happens - The Happy Buddha
- Untethered Soul - Michael Singer

7

Communicate with yourself

Fear & growth

Fear is one of the first communication channels with yourself, from a subconscious and emotional level. Because our current mode of operation is getting us to feel stuck and stressed, we need to do things differently. But change brings about stress, which our body responds to as fear, as our subconscious mind doesn't like uncertainty. Fear is really interesting and it's actually a great teacher—when paying attention to fear arising, it's a great mirror and can emphasise your understanding of yourself. So, let's dive in deeper and become aware of what fear can teach you and why it's important you're aware of it.

Fear comes from the amygdala part of your brain, the part where your emotions stem from. The amygdala is very powerful and triggers our first response to any challenging situation, this is the freeze, fight, or flight response, activating your sympathetic nervous system. You feel stressed, nervous and unsure. But at a certain point your rationale, located in your prefrontal cortex, takes over. This is the point where you can adjust and control your emotions.

When fear arises, which in itself is okay and of course can be triggered in different ways for each person, try not to act straight away on this freeze, fight, flight response (which is actually a reaction, and not an action), but instead just observe. You can't fight or counteract this response, but you can deal with it proactively with a better outcome for yourself. And when your initial impulse to react has subsided, you can readjust based on what works best for you.

Let's say you want to be a confident presenter, and this is a very useful example. Not only have I gone through this process myself, but public speaking remains fear number one in our society. When you're about to appear in front of your audience, you feel the nerves racing through your veins and you'd prefer running away and hiding in a corner. However, if you let the fear subside (deep breaths always calm the sympathetic nervous system) you can and need to remind yourself of the positives; why you want to be heard, how much you'll learn from this opportunity and what contribution you can deliver to your listeners. You then work from a state that supports you, not one that feels burdening and overwhelming.

Don't let fear sabotage you. You can take control of the situation. You just didn't know how fear works and how you can deal with it. Look at it from a positive viewpoint, know what's important to you and you'll be able to act and not react.

Enjoy the challenge, to me that's the epitome of having a growth mindset. And one thing I always tell myself when life gets challenging, which lately happens a lot around building my business, is: if it was easy, it wasn't worth it. I'll explain it through an analogy from my life: I practice Korean martial arts and after about 15 years of training in three different arts I am now in the final stages of preparing for my first black belt exam. Do you think if that assessment was going to be a breeze, I'd feel good about it? What if my instructor, who also happens to be my husband, would just hand me that belt without any effort from my side? Of course, I wouldn't accept it, it's something you must work for, earn, and be proud of. The same goes for the challenge of life, it's not supposed to be easy. Be open to the experience and enjoy the learning these challenges bring about.

As mentioned, we are wired for negativity, so when fear shows up, focus on the positives. You can have a rational conversation with fear, and you'll realise it's only a thought, and most likely not real as your mind has created these stories to quickly interpret new situations.

TIME TO UNCLOG

Again, let's start simply by first off creating awareness of our fear. Already knowing what's going on and exploring it, you're learning a lot about yourself. This way you can adapt and do what's right for you, in a positive and supportive way.

- **Reframe**: As described above, when fear arises (which mainly shows up in the form of avoidance for example procrastination or making a difficult decision), take a deep breath to calm your nervous system and then reframe the situation. Think about your goals and align the situation in a positive way.

- **Visualise the outcome**: This proven method will make you see the outcome is possible. By imagining it, you're tricking your brain into seeing the outcome that will automatically help you move forward. If you can't visualise it's possible, it's much harder to work towards the outcome.

- **Rationalise the fear**: When really facing a challenging moment, I'd suggest this exercise from Tim Ferriss. He suggests delving deeper to help you reframe in a more structured manner and reducing the stress. It's a way to identify all the bad things that could happen to you and will diminish your fear of taking action. Grab a piece of paper and let's begin.

- Start off with a checklist that outlines what could happen:

    1. Define - What are the worst things that could happen?
    2. Prevent - How do I prevent each of those things from happening?
    3. Repair - If the worst happens, how can I fix it?

- Make a list of the possible advantages if you succeed or even only partially succeed.

- Make a list of the disadvantages of your inaction. In other words, if you avoid doing theses thing what might you miss out on?

This exercise is very helpful and inspires you to take action by completely reframing the situation from a point of fear to a point where you're seeing the positive potential.

How does this support unclogging?

Unclogging requires change and change leads to fear. Understanding how fear works and how you can manage it will make moving from a clogged state to an unclogged state much easier.

Your language

The language you use offers another fascinating insight into how you approach and perceive the world. It's not only an indicator, but it also has a huge effect on your behaviour. Where fear is a strong emotional response, your language stems more from your rationale self. It's bringing awareness to your thoughts.

It's so important to be aware of your language. The words you choose dictate the outcome. If we thus want to see a different outcome, it's essential we have sufficient knowledge about this. For example, if you're always telling yourself you can't do a cartwheel, do you think you'll ever be able to do one? As Dr. Andrew Newberg states in *Words Can Change Your Brain*: "*Language shapes our behaviour and each word we use is imbued with multitudes of personal meaning. The right words spoken in the right way can bring us love, money, and respect, while the wrong words—or even the right words spoken in the wrong way — can lead a country to war. We must carefully orchestrate our speech if we want to achieve our goals and bring our dreams to fruition.*"

> Where fear is a strong emotional response, your language stems more from your rationale self. It's bringing awareness to your thoughts.

The field of brain science shows us you can control and change your thoughts and emphasises what a powerful tool language is. Fascinating research by Debi Roberson et all points out that what we can't describe we also can't see. The Himba Tribe in Namibia evidently can't distinguish between the colours blue and green. Not only do they not have a word to describe the colour blue, but they also can't point out a blue square surrounded by green squares. They can, however, distinguish between different shades of green a lot better than you and I can. What this tells us, is that how we describe the world is how we perceive it and vice versa.

Communication expert Michael Grinder (in personal training) points out that it's our responsibility to increase our vocabulary. If you can describe it, you can also observe it. If you don't have a word for it, how can you experience it? Language raises your awareness and your perception of your environment. And remember, we can choose our reality based on what we focus on.

Negative labelling

Imagine you have the tendency to label things in a negative way, do you think you'll be able to view your world in a positive way? Our society is full of negative clichés and they're not helping us at all. In Part I of this book we already talked about being busy and that this seems the norm, but then we worry about our stress levels and complain we never have enough time. Isn't that a self-fulfilling prophecy? I have banned the word 'busy' from my vocabulary. Because when I ask someone *"How've you been?"* and they respond with busy, I even wonder what that means. Have you enjoyed being busy? Or are you saying you're stressed? Or are you implying an excuse for not catching up with me sooner? Or do you like justifying yourself? I have no idea. After thinking about it, I replaced the word 'busy' with 'productive'. For me, that means I've been happily working towards my goals, focused and with intention.

Here are some words you can use to replace the word 'busy' with:

- Productive
- Flourishing
- Engaged
- Occupied
- Captivated
- Focused
- Thriving
- Involved

Which one resonates with you?

It's important to pay attention to the words you choose and use. Other words to change are:

- 'I want' instead of 'I should' or 'I need'. I strongly believe in the power of choice and taking personal responsibility (more on that in Part III). By rephrasing your sentence to 'I want' changes your entire attitude.

- 'Challenges' instead of 'problems'. This one I learned from one of my first (and best) bosses. I was 18 and working in retail, customer service, and whenever I'd approach him with an issue and said *"Michel, we have a problem"*, he would always correct me and say that we never have problems, we only have challenges. This way you can tackle it from a perspective that you can solve and handle it. At this point, you may have already realised I haven't used the word problem in this book either.

- 'Learnings' instead of 'failures'. As Thomas Edison pointed out *"I haven't failed— I've just found 10,000 ways that won't work."*

- Another really good option is finishing a sentence with 'yet'. My personal favourite: I can't do a cartwheel 'yet'.

The power of your thoughts

What about your own narrative? How do you talk to yourself? Have you ever wondered how it affects you?

In Dr. Masaru Emoto's fascinating book *Hidden Messages in Water*, the researcher shows the visual evidence of the following discovery. Using high-speed photography; frozen water crystals show significantly different patterns depending on what type of thoughts it's been subjected to. Where water, before freezing, has been subjected to loving and kind words, the crystals showed beautiful, colourful and well-formed snowflake structures. While water subjected to negativity and hate, showed unformed, irregular and rough patterns.

Recently, many people on social media did the 4-week rice experiment, which is also based on Dr. Emoto's work. You can easily try this one for yourself; put cooked rice in three different glass jars and cover them. For the duration of the experiment, you say nice and loving words to one jar, degrading and mean words to another jar and you ignore the third jar. You will be astonished at what rate the rice will rot and grow mould.

Your internal dialogue has a profound effect on your attitude, performance, and fulfillment in life. We all have this negative self-talk, but you have to start building yourself up. Saying negative things to yourself is not doing you any good. You need to support yourself, back yourself, always. That's your responsibility. Of course, getting acknowledgement, praise or kindness from others is helpful and feels really good. But what if you didn't even have to rely on that? You can't sit, wait and hope for the world to give that to you, while you are capable of doing so yourself. And why are you so nice to your loved ones, but not to yourself?

You can have two different types of thoughts: the ones that build you up or the ones that break you down. Negative thoughts are hugely detrimental to your wellbeing, it's time to focus on the positive ones.

TIME TO UNCLOG

It's clear that it's vital to work towards a supportive positive inner voice and here's how you can start:

- **Compliment yourself:** Give yourself a compliment at the end of every day. What have you done well? What are you proud of? This is a very simple step toward building yourself up.

- **Stop using auto responses:** What clichés do you use that don't support your state of mind? Mondayitis, another day another dollar, it is what it is? You now know better and it's time to stop using those clichés. Describe your world in a different way.

- **Change your vocabulary:** Over the next week or so write down any of the negative words you tend to use and reframe them. Keep this list with you until you've noticed the positive effect it's yielded.

- **Specify your emotions:** Describe your emotions more specifically, not out of habit. Pick an emotion you're challenged with and one you're using a lot for describing how you're feeling. Let's take anxious as an example. Write down 10 words on a scale of 1 to 10 in severity to describe this emotion. Unsure might be on 2 or 3, while nervous can be on 5, and anxious on 9 and panic on 10. Now if you always use 'anxious' to describe how you're feeling, while actually, you're feeling nervous, you've internally dramatised it for yourself. Also, by labelling it in the same manner, your mind can't differentiate between the different emotions, and your mind will associate it with previous situations of anxiety and will already pre-empt feeling that way. Use different descriptions of emotions to specify how you're actually feeling at the moment, don't sabotage yourself by generalising your emotions.

How does this support unclogging?

To be in control of your life it's essential being able to support yourself. The language you use is the key indicator here. By being able to describe your world in a more positive and supportive way, you'll be able to feel a lot less clogged.

Talk to yourself

I want to take the concept of thought awareness one step further; for you to really understand yourself better, you have to be able to communicate with yourself. I'm not referring to the negative self-talk, that's a monologue anyway. You need to engage in a real conversation. Asking yourself on a daily basis what you need or how you're feeling are great and simple ways to check in with yourself and then use that knowledge to adjust if necessary. To have an honest conversation with yourself is the single most important aspect of working from the inside out. Not allowing yourself from getting caught up by what others need, you first of all need to know what you need.

Be honest

As you're making progress with the ability to communicate with yourself, it's now also time to be honest with yourself. Many clients of mine will always be slightly apprehensive or defensive when certain challenging aspects of how they operate are being discussed. When you notice defending yourself by saying: *"that's what I always do"* or *"that just seems to work for me"*, ask yourself: is that really true?

It's very dangerous describing yourself in a factual way that limits you from opportunities for growth. Never state yourself in a factual way that comes from a fixed mindset. A very limiting example is stating *"oh, but I'm stubborn because I'm a Taurus"*.

My husband Frank, for example, has been diagnosed with dyslexia in his teens. Finding the right words or thinking on the spot isn't something that comes naturally to him. When he did the Gallup Strength Assessment, it came to no surprise that communication showed up at the bottom end. However, for him to state *"I can't write emails well"* or *"I always have trouble with making phone calls"*, is limiting his own opportunity for growth. When we discussed this, it was eye-opening for him. He has now even changed the sentence from *"I am dyslexic"* to *"I have dyslexic characteristics"*.

Do you remember from the previous chapter when we discussed emotional clarity, how important it is not limiting yourself to one interpretation of a situation? The same accounts for how you perceive yourself, it's never set in stone or 'always'. With my husband we could see as soon as he's explaining his passion for martial arts or teaching, he wasn't being challenged by his communication capability at all. It's key to become aware of that for yourself and then figure out a way that best works for you.

Don't ever feel completely stuck. We always have available skills in our arsenal to help us on our way. We already are somewhere on the scale of progress when addressing a challenge. If you think about the things you're challenged with; rate yourself on a scale of 1-10 of how far you've progressed. We are never a 1; we already have some qualities and experiences available when starting off. Stay focused on what you already have, as that will help you see it's possible and you can do this.

Stop changing yourself

Your attitude toward bringing in affect change is essential. An important question to ask yourself is if you're changing yourself or improving your situation?

Think back of your core philosophy, strengths and skills that make up who you are; you wouldn't want to change this. You might want to improve on them, but at the core of all, you don't want to change this. Why would you want to be someone completely different anyway?

Take for example my client Marie who always does what others might label as a lot of research before making a final decision. We had a conversation about this as it was sometimes causing her frustration that it took her a considerate amount of time to make a decision, as she was analysing all imaginable options. She wished that making decisions would come easier to her rather than constantly outweighing possible options. Sometimes she would even envy the people just doing things spontaneously. But I challenged her on the question if she really wanted to change this. Yes, we agreed sometimes her tendency of analysing choices would lead to overanalysing and personal frustration. But this is however also how she takes care of others. Contemplating, considering different options and caring for others is one of her core strengths (whether finding a brunch place that suits everyone or deciding on a retirement home for her aunt). For Marie, it's very important allowing herself to work through the options and wishing that she could make an instant choice would not work for her. It wouldn't align with who she is and it most likely would make her feel very confused or even anxious.

> **It's important to support yourself with who you are, and never buy into the thoughts that you should be anyone else.**

It's important to support yourself with who you are, and never buy into the thoughts that you should be anyone else.

TIME TO UNCLOG

To become even more aware of the thoughts that occupy your mind and understand what you really need, have a look at these tools you can start implementing.

- **Check in with yourself**: Ask yourself every morning; How do I feel and how do I want to feel? Then figure out how you're going to achieve this by taking specific actions. If you ask yourself these questions, everything you want and need to do that day becomes clearer. It sets you up for a great day.

- **Notice your defensive attitude**: Become aware of when you're defending yourself or justifying your challenges in a self-limiting way. Is that actually true? Write down a list of 5 to 10 situations where this wasn't the case. This will help with the elimination of your fixed mindset.

- **Stop changing yourself**: Create an attitude of 'growth', and not one of constantly 'more'. It's a minor adjustment but has a potentially large effect. It's never the aim to change yourself and constantly setting goals or improving what you're naturally NOT good at. Aim at developing yourself, especially by utilising your strengths, and at the same time improving the situation. Be happy with what you have, while pursuing what you want.

How does this support unclogging?

To be real with yourself and continuously exploring yourself, rather than identifying yourself as a fixed entity will set you up with resilience. A flexible mindset about your own being, helps you adapt when challenges come your way. This way you can unclog.

Key points

- Stress is a fear-based subconscious response and can't be eliminated but can be managed.
- Changing your language has a profound impact on your world.
- Negative self-talk is the worst form of self-sabotage.
- It's essential to have honest conversations with yourself.

Implementation

Create awareness of your thoughts and needs through daily check ins:

- What do I need and what am I going to do to fulfil it?
- How am I feeling and how do I want to feel at the end of the day?
- Change your stereotypical and negative labelling of situations and emotions.

Further learning

- Mindset - Carol Dweck
- Breaking the Habit of Being Yourself - Joe Dispenza
- Change Your Language, Change Your Life - Wayne Dwyer
- A Life of Being, Doing and Having Enough - Wayne Muller
- Gifts of Imperfection - Brene Brown
- I Hope I Screw This Up - Kyle Cease
- Be Fearless - Jonathan Alpert

PART III
Redo

This is the part of the process where you:

Take responsibility and put into action
what you know about yourself

Assess your surroundings for self-reflection

Align your actions with your beliefs

Commit to consistent practice

8

Evaluate

"We are what we repeatedly do."
— Aristotle

Real vs ideal

To implement what we know about ourselves, our first step is to evaluate. Part II of this book ended with the importance of starting to have honest conversations with yourself for you to determine what you need and want. But also, to become more positive in your thoughts, emotions and even your language so your perception changes into something that supports you better. With this knowledge, it's time to continue with ways to put this into action.

The first step to take is to evaluate what's going on in your life and separating your real from your ideal self. As previously mentioned, it's important not to want to change yourself. And if you focus on an ideal version of yourself, how you want to be, you're not supporting yourself. When putting what you've learned about yourself into action, your life feels easier and more in flow as you're accepting your real self and who you actually are. It's how we're thinking, feeling, perceiving, and acting. As you're going into the redoing part of the process, it's important to have this clarity. We all want to get the most out of life, whatever that means to us on an individual level. But as we set our goals and we're working to improve our situation, it's important to let go of the high expectations. You probably overestimate your capabilities or the future and when your expectations aren't met, you feel deflated and frustrated. And straight away you're trapped in your old cycle of getting clogged. The most common way of getting ourselves in trouble because of our ideal self is how we spend our time. Let's see how this affects us.

Time

We have bad judgement when it comes to how we actually spend our time. Erik Helzer and his colleague Shai Davidai, of Princeton's Woodrow Wilson School of Public and International Affairs, have been studying people's perceptions of how they use their time. In one study, they asked participants on a Friday how they would spend their weekends. On Monday, they followed up to see how that time was actually spent. Participants who said they were going to do restorative activities—like reading a book or hiking in the woods—actually did things like binge watching tv. This leads to an interesting twist in our perception; we think we don't have free time when we actually do. We sabotage ourselves as we do other activities than that we want to be doing, and this leisure time doesn't register as restorative. And apparently we do a lot of it; we spend about three to five hours watching tv a day.

Remember my story of the Sunday afternoon on the sofa with five things I wanted to do? Of course, that wasn't going to work for me and stressed me out, while that was even my leisure time. This is how we're sabotaging ourselves. Time is our most precious resource; you're never getting it back. It's so important we are intentional about how we're spending our time.

*"It's not that we have a short time to live,
but that we waste much of it."*
– SENECA, ON THE SHORTNESS OF LIFE.

A Forbes article by Dan Pontefract outlines several studies that show how busy and occupied we are. We are now spending five hours a day on our mobile phones. He described that our work ethics give us the impression we always need to be 'on' and we constantly strive for high productivity. Other research that Pontefract outlines, states that the average office worker now receives 121 emails a day we check our phones on average once every 12 minutes or over 80 times a day.

We think we don't have enough time, but actually, we do. It's up to you to decide how you want to spend your time. Either your day runs you, or you run your day. Be intentional with how you spend your time. Be in control, but you can only do that when you're real with yourself. Because remember, quantitively we're not busier, but qualitatively we are.

TIME TO UNCLOG

It's in your control how you spend your time. To become more intentional where you focus your energy, I'd like to suggest starting here:

- **Start and finish the day with abundance**: Don't sabotage yourself as you start your day by having a to-do-list that isn't even accomplishable or complaining you haven't had enough sleep. Ensure you set yourself up with excitement and a positive attitude, even if it's as simple as your list of three things you're grateful for. And don't end the day by thinking about what you didn't accomplish. Instead, focus on input rather than output; what did you learn today or what was the highlight of your day?

- **Be realistic with your tasks and commitments**: When making a to-do-list; is this really going to work for you and fill you with joy? Is it in line with what you want to focus on? Don't make a list that sets you up for failure. I know how it is to have high standards, but only use them when it's in line with your real self—know when it adds value and when it doesn't. For me, I consciously make a decision to ensure my house is spotless, but I'm happy to forfeit some exercise time.

How does this support unclogging?

Being realistic about your time will help you align your achievements with your expectations. This intention will result in you spending time the way you want, and not under pressure. You'll be in control.

Individual Balance Point

Life is constantly adjusting between two opposing energies. In nature, we always strive for balance. The same principle applies when wanting to stay unclogged. Going back to our ecosystem example from earlier on, let's look at the individual tree again. On one hand, it needs to be strong and grounded, but also not too rigid that it snaps during a storm. And whether it's a palm tree or a solid oak, both need to be strong, yet flexible.

The same goes for you; it's important to constantly seek balance. We all strive for structure but also freedom. It's important to be clear and determined, yet adaptable and flexible. It's finding your sweet spot; knowing at that moment what works best for you. That moment in time, I refer to as your Individual Balance Point (IBP) and you are the only one who knows that point.

Let's say you don't feel like exercising. Normally you're really disciplined, but today you're not in the mood for exercise. It could be you are a bit lazy and need to push through, and you'll feel better afterwards. Or perhaps you've been very occupied this week and your body is actually in need of some rest. If you'll push through you might even feel more exhausted rather than energised. Being able to point out, at that moment what it is you actually need, is entirely up to you. And as your knowledge about yourself increases through the work in the rethinking process, identifying this point only becomes easier.

Focus on your strengths and use them to the best of your ability, but don't overuse them or rely on one strength too much. For me, it's about wanting the best. I strive for excellence, and that's important to me, but if

I go in overdrive, I'm in perfectionism mode. And that is sabotaging me from moving forward. At that point, I feel bogged down and not in flow. To stay unclogged it's important to know your Individual Balance Point.

It's of utmost importance knowing where you're sitting on the scale. One point on the scale is supporting you to be your best, in line with who you are, the other is limiting you from moving forward. Being aware of your sweet spot, your IBP, is going to make all the difference in how you adapt and make situations work for you. Prior to knowing this, you would've maybe withdrawn or pushed through, but now you can create the clarity from within, so you know exactly what to do.

Know when it's too much

Even though in our society we're surrounded by information overload, I do want to highlight that this is also a case of a double-edged sword. We know that information overload can lead to confusion, but it's important noting that confusion doesn't only stem from too much information but also not having sufficient information. Knowledge can both save and burden us.

Know when it's too much. Former US Secretary of State Colin Powell said: *"I can make a decision with 30 percent of the information. Anything more than 80 is too much."* For him, that's what works. It's up to you to figure out what's enough, but also to identify what information adds value and what doesn't. Some information is noise, while other parts are the advantages of our evolving society. And what may be noise to me, may very well not be noise to you. You might be a coffee enthusiast and thrive on all the options at Starbucks, and I might have no clue and only become confused by all the available options.

> **Knowledge can both save and burden us.**

It's all about knowing your 'enough' and having trust in the fact of not having to know everything, so you can decide what works for you. It's like going to the supermarket not knowing what to eat and not knowing what you have at home; all the 42,000 different products on the shelves leave you with multiple options and can be overwhelming. But if you know you want to eat Italian and you still have some sauce and parmesan at home, you then know you only have to get some vegetables and pasta when shopping. Make sure you equip yourself with the knowledge of what you need. It's finding that balance and checking in with yourself to determine what it really is you need.

TIME TO UNCLOG

What's your 'enough'? Where do you operate best? And are you aware of when you're not? Bringing attention to the moments where things aren't working well are amazing learning opportunities.

- **Awareness of overusing your strengths**: Go back to your strengths and what you're naturally good at; which strength do you tend to overuse that causes you to feel stressed, rather than in flow (clogged or unclogged)? Find examples where you were operating in your sweet spot, your IBP, a balance between utilising it fully, but without overuse.

- **Awareness of information consumption**: As you go through your everyday life, take the occasional moment to evaluate whether the information stream coming to you is of value. Think emails, social media, online shopping, advertising, news. Become intentional about what you consume.

EVALUATE

How does this support unclogging?

Constantly seeking to find your own balance and knowing what noise is to you, is essential in getting and staying unclogged. This way you'll have the flexibility to adapt when unexpected things come your way.

Your responsibility

> *"If you don't make time for exercise, you'll probably have to make time for illness."*
> – ROBIN SHARMA

Taking ownership is one of the key aspects of leading yourself. You need to ensure you've figured out what to focus on. How can you manage your life if you don't? Think about leading a high performing team. If you're their leader, you need to be crystal clear on the vision you have, so they can align, come together and do their best work. The same accounts for your own life. You need to lead yourself from a place of clarity. Show up as that leader, in line with your values and your strengths. Then it's your job to apply your knowledge consistently.

The single most effective way of taking control of your life is to stop making excuses. If you find yourself saying things like *"I don't have the time"*, how are you going to make the changes in your life that you're craving for? Take control and consider what you can do differently. You need to be willing to learn, read and grow to make the changes. You either decide to change your situation or change your wants.

Everything in your life is the way it is because you choose so. Are you ready for the change? *"The payoffs for having a blank unwillingness sheet are monumental"* said Wayne Dwyer in his book *Excuses Begone!* If there's nothing you're not willing to do, with no excuses and no one to blame, everything becomes a possibility. For different results, different actions are required. If you want your life to be different, you first have to be willing to do things differently. Do the hard stuff. Don't take the short-cuts. You know the challenges are an opportunity for growth due to your positive mindset and with the intention you've set why this is important to you. Then go and work on it.

TIME TO UNCLOG

Now it's time for you to take ownership of your life, to take full control. It's your life and how you experience it is within your own internal power. You just need to know how.

- **Be intentional with your actions**: What can you give up to ensure you have more time on hand? Looking at your commitments, are they in line with what you're working towards? But also assess whether you spend your time intentionally to support your values and goals.

- **Know your excuses**: Where do you tend to make excuses? Which area of your life have you been struggling with the most? Can you identify the excuses you tend to make? I realise this is a more confronting question, but you've already come a long way in this process, and I know by now you'll be able to give yourself an honest answer.

How does this support unclogging?

Your life is your drain and it's your responsibility to take care of it. The current state of your life is because of your own actions and being aware of it and willing to go and work on it will make all the difference in your unclogging process.

Key points

- Be realistic with your goals and expectations and spend your time intentionally.
- Always strive to find your Individual Balance Point at any given moment.
- Stop with the excuses and be willing to take ownership and lead yourself to make the changes happen.

Implementation

To work towards your balance point:

- Take your top 3-5 strengths and determine what in specific is your optimum mode of operating.
- Map out what's of value to you in your life and what is noise.
- Stay open, be willing and commit to an unclogged life.

Further learning

- Excuses Begone! - Dr. Wayne W. Dyer
- Extreme Ownership - Jocko Willink

Let go

―――

"The thing you surrender becomes your power."
− Wayne Dwyer

What to let go of

We need to build on our unquestionable ability to eliminate. During the rethinking phase we've already let go of negativity and in the previous chapter, we've started to identify and let go of what noise is to us. But there's more to let go of. As the more you let go of, the easier your life becomes and the more you can emphasise what matters most to you.

Aiming for simplicity is a challenging task, as you need to know what to let go of. In this chapter, we'll cover letting go from an internal perspective as well as the external. Both have a profound effect and through my years of studying and experience in this area, I know that aiming to let go in both areas magnifies the effect.

Patrick Rhone in his book *Enough* says it perfectly:

"Enough comes from trying things out. It comes from challenging your preconceptions. It comes from having less, trying more, then reducing to find out what is just right. It comes from letting go of your fear of less. It comes from letting go of the false security of more. It also comes from having more, losing it all, and finding out what need really is. Enough is hard work.

To get there, one must let go of what-ifs, conjectures, assumptions, guesses, and half-truths. One must overcome fear, gluttony, self-doubt, and thoughts of grandeur. One must ask hard questions to find harder answers.

But, please keep in mind, even that changes. Just as the wire walker must make slight adjustments to constantly changing conditions, so must you.

The goal, then, is not to find what is or will be enough forever. That is impossible. The goal is to discover the tools and strategies you need to find what is enough for you right now and provide the flexibility to adjust as the conditions change."

In Brene Brown's first book *The Gifts of Imperfection* she has a fantastic list of what to let go of to live your best life. These are the barriers to your happiness. Think back to your answers in Chapter 6 about how you perceive happiness and what limits you from having that happiness as we go through these items.

1. **What people think** - not being able to let go of this, limits you from being yourself as you're being influenced by what people think.
2. **Perfectionism** - always aiming to meet your high expectations doesn't allow you to be kind to yourself.
3. **Numbing** - when things get challenging and you avoid rather than tackle them, you're not building your resilience.
4. **Scarcity** - don't fear the future and stop focussing on what you don't have, cultivate contentment through gratitude.
5. **The need for certainty** - the world is not going to give you what you need or go according to your plans, have an open mind.

6. **Comparison** - you are uniquely you as we've established in Chapter 5 and there's no need to compare yourself with others, we are all on our own journey.
7. **Productivity as self-worth** – we've discussed lots of this already, but to be happy in life it's essential to also enjoy life and take it all in.
8. **Anxiety as a lifestyle** - our world is so hectic, and this entire book is about not getting trapped in it.
9. **Self-doubt and 'supposed to'** - do what fills you with joy and what's in line with your philosophy, give purpose to everything you do.
10. **Being in control all the time** - don't take life so seriously, let loose a little.

Be okay to ask yourself the hard questions - what can I let go of, what am I willing to uncover? We need to challenge ourselves on the assumptions and beliefs we have (RETHINK). Defining enough for you, at this moment, is scary, extremely liberating, empowering and everything in between. But it's an amazing process to go through; ask yourself if you're ready for the challenge.

TIME TO UNCLOG

It's now time for the challenge and start building your 'letting go' muscle.

- **Identify your barriers**: For each of the ten barriers on Brene Brown's list, rate them from 1 to 10, 10 being this not an issue for you at all. At the lowest three scores, write down three actions you can take to limit the barriers even more.

- **Work on your growth mindset**: How are you feeling about letting go? Is it something that comes easy to you or do you tend to be more rigid? Think back about having a growth mindset and understand why life feels challenging for you. The only way to get there is to let go of what isn't working for you.

How does this support unclogging?

Letting go of barriers that are in the way of your happiness is the epitome of unclogging. To know what challenges you the most, is essential for your growth. Stop sabotaging yourself and simplify.

Assess your environment

Now let's focus on your physical environment. This is your outer circle; this is what you surround yourself with. If you don't give this the attention and intention it needs, it will clog you up. Your physical environment can keep you stuck in the past or too focused on the future. Letting go of items that don't represent who you are at this moment, or what you don't need anymore, is not only liberating but also extremely helpful toward creating the life you want.

Now it's time to go through your stuff and decide what to keep or not to keep. A lot of very helpful books about the topic of minimalism are available and I'll list my favourites at the end of this chapter. However, the one thing I want to first off mention is that it has to work for you. It's not about living frugally or with limitations, it's about emphasising what matters most. What matters most to you, not to anyone else. Going through this physical process will enhance what you've learned about yourself, especially being real with yourself. A lot of the items we have in our life relate to an ideal version of ourselves (books that we haven't read yet, jeans we don't fit in anymore, camping gear we haven't used for years). Minimalism is the physical manifestation of self-awareness and living in the now. Minimalism is a mirror, a tool for acceptance, gratitude and enough. A tool to learn about ourselves.

There are many different ways to approach this, but here are some important essentials:

- **Start small**: The one thing I never want to do is to overwhelm you. Start with a simple area, the easy stuff like a junk drawer or simply by eliminating one item a day. My mum did the latter for over a year and it made such an impact on her, she just kept going. It worked for her.

- **Know your reasons**: Don't start this for my sake but be intentional of why decluttering would help you. Do you want to feel lighter?

Waste less time finding things or maintaining your home? Or do you want to learn more about yourself in a practical way?

- **Set rules for yourself**: There're a few different ways you can challenge yourself to start off with:

    o One in, two out of the same type of item. If you buy a new jacket, then two jackets need to go. This is my personal favourite as it makes you so mindful of buying something new as two items then need to go.

    o For a month; 1st day 1 item out, 2nd day 2 items out, etc. See if you can even go for longer, but it's a great start.

    o Buy nothing for 2 months, except food and fuel. You'll soon realise you've got everything you need.

    o If an item hasn't been used for the last 6-12 months, it must go. We keep so much unnecessary stuff for 'what if' moments and they're not even useful. If and when that moment comes, we can always be resourceful.

    o Box it up and unpack only what you need. What hasn't been used after X months goes. Do this per area of the house of course. I did it with kitchen gear and it worked really well.

    o Capsule your wardrobe - have only a limited number of items of clothing for a season. Courtney Carver from Project 333 lives by her rule of 33 items for three months, then she switches them. I do change my wardrobe every three months, so I've got 'new' stuff every season. The 33 items were however too limiting for me personally but a great eyeopener. I got rid of most of my jewellery though as I realised, I wasn't wearing them at all.

o One location for one type of item and that's it. Whatever doesn't fit in the designated area goes. This works well for books, shoes, or nail polishes. Don't let things overflow to other areas of your house.

All beginnings are hard, but as soon as you start you realise it's not that challenging. As I said, begin with the easy stuff and start small, that builds your 'letting go' muscle and you can later move on to the more challenging stuff. My decluttering journey happened over the space of 12-18 months and reflecting back on it, it was about four phases.

Phase 1 was all the junk and made me wonder why on earth was this in our house. This was quite an easy start.
Phase 2 was letting go of the useful items, but were clearly never used by us; think kitchen gadgets or camping gear.
Phase 3 got quite a lot more challenging; things that I really liked but wasn't using; like my digital SLR camera, a pair of shoes that didn't match anything, or a pair of really expensive glasses that were too heavy to wear and gave me a headache within a few hours.
Phase 4 was a more gradual and slower moving phase, that involved eliminating items I thought were going to add value to my life but with a second assessment, I realised I could let go of them too (expensive jewellery for instance—I could wear it, I thought it was beautiful, but then never ended up wearing it).

Please don't get discouraged by the length or the intensity of my journey. This is what I did and what worked for me. The most important part is for you to enjoy the process as you'll learn what matters most to you. Define what clutter is to you and remove everything that fits that definition. You're not saying no but saying yes to what's important to you. You're getting back more than you're giving up.

Here are benefits that all minimalists describe, and it certainly also applies to me:

- You become more conscious of how you spend your resources. Whether it's money or time. This awareness supports you in other areas too.

- You are less stressed and overwhelmed. The areas in your home reflect what they need to reflect, and they don't remind you of what is or what could be. You can be in the present.

- You cultivate contentment. You realise you have everything you need and your desire for fixing or for more diminishes as you continue decluttering. Joshua Becker in his book *The More of Less* puts it beautifully; *"owning less is great, even better yet is wanting less"*.

- You create space for emotions. Many people are worried about getting rid of memorabilia. But instead of having everything in a box in the garage, what if you have the three most important items actually showcased in your home.

- You remove negativity. Even though some items are not in the way, they still take up mental space and probably do not add to positivity. Think back to my digital SLR camera; it was never in the way, but I felt I was obliged to use it.

The environment you live in affects your mental state, so it's your responsibility to take care of that too.

Maintain

Decluttering is not a simple and one-shot fix. It's a different attitude to constantly assessing what you need and what's of value to you. It's creating a habit of tidying up. I was taught this as a kid, and it comes naturally to me. And I know this really doesn't sound sexy, but it really makes all the difference in the world. It shows how proud you are of your space and that you're willing to put in the work for it. Just the other day I had the pleasure of meeting the guy who built our house three decades ago. He randomly showed up, but I was proudly showing him my house, without the internal desire to quickly tidy up. There was nothing (besides a few notes and books on my desk) on any of the surface areas. I'm proud to say that my space is a physical representation of me.

Create a positive space

By decluttering you're giving room and purpose to the items you keep. You're highlighting them, spotlight if you will. My mum had two shopping baskets full of scarfs, she didn't even know she had all of them. Most of them were given to her by her sister who now passed away. Decluttering the emotional stuff is hard. Make it your responsibility ensuring your association with them are positive (a few items beautifully displayed in your home or given to a family member) and not negative (sitting in boxes in the garage and feeling heavy). By reducing the number of items, you can literally give them a better spot in your life, one they deserve. It gives greater value to the memories attached to them, rather than keeping all of them tucked away somewhere.

We need to create space for ourselves. Not only is it visually pleasing and provides clarity, but it also releases us from negativity. So many of our belongings hold us stuck in the past, wishing for a potential future or holding expectations that others have of us. But by holding on to it, we subconsciously decide to keep that negativity around us, rather than accepting where and who we are in this moment.

Altogether it creates the atmosphere you desire. Make your environment as beautiful, calm and spacious as you need it to be. Whether you create it in line with strict Japanese organisation (Marie Kondo), or warm Danish cosiness (Hygge) or some Dutch pragmatism and efficiency (me); I know you'll create your own style, in line with your personal beliefs.

As a final note; please consider donating the useful items you're getting rid of. By giving it away and sharing it with others, makes you realise it's of much better use where it ends up rather than in a box or a wardrobe at your home.

TIME TO UNCLOG

Time to start clearing out some of your clutter. I know starting this can be challenging, but believe me, it'll be worth it. Just make sure you do it your way.

- **Pick a challenge that suits you**: Which decluttering challenge would you like to start with? It's important to pick something that resonates with you. Perhaps you're one that likes to see big results and you want to dive all in, or you might be the slow starter building up momentum.

- **Know your reasons**: What do you consider the main benefits of decluttering? Consider the benefits of letting go vs the disadvantages of holding on.

- **Digital declutter**: Also, consider reducing the amount of useless (to you) information you consume. Link the previous chapter with this and perhaps you can start unsubscribing from email newsletters. And if only 1 in the 20 you receive from that business adds value, I'd still say let go—focus on the 19 times it didn't.

- **Get creative and try**: What can simplify your life that you haven't thought of yet? I'm not saying you should go for this, but as soon as I decided to go for my pixie haircut, my hair products (styling, shampoo, equipment) reduced with 90%. Let's be creative and have some fun here. Don't be afraid of something new, and if it doesn't work, you can always reinstate it. Yes, you might need to spend a bit of money replacing the items you got rid of, but 9 out of 10 times you won't want to go back.

How does this support unclogging?

Creating space to emphasise what matters most is one of the most powerful concepts of unclogging. Have a drain that's open and spacious, one that's content and functioning well without the extra baggage. Your physical space reflects the choices you make.

Say no

One of the best words you need to be able to use is 'no'. When you're clear on your intentions, values, and goals; anything that doesn't align with them requires a 'no'. Learn to say 'no' and stay true to yourself. Stick to your guns. However, this is easier said than done. Like most of us, we want to help others, be part of something and, albeit a bit selfish, feel appreciated. It's in our altruistic nature to give in and say yes to incoming requests. But therein lies the big danger of getting clogged again, by subconsciously or unintentionally letting things enter your life that doesn't add value.

> Justifying is trying to convince the other party, explaining is outlining your point without a response needed.

As my wonderful British friend says: *"I need to channel my inner Dutch-ness"*. Be okay with being direct. Rightfully, for me, that's a bit easier as I've inherited that with my Dutch upbringing. But in all seriousness, it's always better for both parties if you're clear on what you need and want to focus on. Being able to articulate that, with respect and understanding, is life changing. There's a difference between explaining it and justifying it. It's time for our society not to feel you have to justify saying no. Justifying is trying to convince the other party, explaining is outlining your point without a response needed. And the clearer you get on what's important to you and how you spend your time, the easier it is to kindly say no.

Feeling guilty

There's one emotion that straight away comes up when we're trying to or have allocated our boundaries. Straight away we tend to feel guilty. Some may feel guilty as they don't want to disappoint others, or a feeling of guilt arises because you're taking care of your own needs. Feeling guilty is a huge challenge for most people.

Here's what I think about feeling guilty; it's one of the most useless emotions. Guilt doesn't serve anyone. You're not changing your decision, so it's not affecting the other party. And in the meantime, you feel miserable about a decision that was going to help you. Remember that it's your responsibility to do what supports you. And this miserable feeling isn't helping anyone, or the situation, and especially not you. Instead feel proud of sticking to your guns, applaud yourself for being clear and protecting your interests. It's like the oxygen masks on the plane; put it on yourself first before you help others. This is the key point of taking care of yourself. In Chapter 11 we'll discuss this in more detail.

To link it back to the previous section; the same goes for saying no to material things. I really had to help my mum with this issue. The minute something has been given to her she accepted it. Well, actually no. You can say no to the giver, but sometimes, and I understand this, it's socially unacceptable or uncomfortable to do so. You don't want to be perceived as ungrateful and especially around people who are not that familiar to you.

> **Feeling guilty; it's one of the most useless emotions.**

Everyone in my inner circle knows very well I don't do gifts. I don't expect any, nor do I give gifts. For me that makes life a lot easier, I find it environmentally friendly, and I gain control over the items that enter my household. Back to my mum, you don't have to use it or keep it. Your home is not a storage place, it's a living space. There's no one benefitting from you keeping things you don't want.

Like all the changes you're implementing, I'd suggest starting small. Perhaps say no to a new committee request or a networking event you don't have the energy for. At this moment it's not adding value to your life. And if it is, fantastic, you'll be one step closer to achieving your goals.

We like being busy; we like being part of something and we're not identifying what we need for ourselves. Of course, we're struggling. You now have the tools to know what's of value, and how to let go of what's not. That will make saying no easier and also with more clarity, and decisions are easier. More on that in the next chapter.

TIME TO UNCLOG

It's now time to create your boundaries and protect yourself. You've identified what does and doesn't work for you, it's now up to you to implement your best strategy and learn to say no.

- **Create a focus for the week**: For this week, write out the 3-5 most important things and assess how full your weekly schedule is. Say no to anything that comes your way that's not enhancing those 3-5 important things.

- **Identify how hard it is for you to say no**: And why is it challenging; do you feel guilty? And do you feel more guilty regarding certain requests compared to others? Decide what you can do differently here.

How does this support unclogging?

Being able to say no with certainty and confidence stems from being internally very clear and completely unclogged. This is the key to creating a different outcome for yourself, from the pressure to ease.

Key points

- To live unclogged and be in control of our environment we have to let go.
- Letting go is the first step putting into practice what you've learned about yourself and will uncover even more.
- Boundaries are essential for you to go where you want to go. Take control and protect what's of value to you.

Implementation

Start creating space by establishing a system for you to let go:

- Challenge yourself on letting go what isn't working internally (based on Brene Brown's list) and,
- Externally, start creating a physical environment that reflects who you are. Implement your chosen declutter strategy.

Further learning

- Gifts of Imperfection - Brene Brown
- Enough - Patrick Rhone
- The More of Less - Joshua Becker
- Everything That Remains - Joshua Fields Millburn & Ryan Nicodemus
- The Joy of Less - Francine Jay
- Boundaries - John Townsend & Henry Cloud

Action

---

*"There can be no happiness if the things we believe
in are different from the things we do."*
— Freya Stark

Intention

Now it's time for action. This is where you implement what you've learned, doings things differently and seeing the change in your life. To be able to unclog in a sustainable and joyful manner, intention is everything. To align your actions with your beliefs, which is really what it comes down to, you need to give it meaning. As soon as it loses purpose for you, or you don't recognise the purpose, it'll feel like pressure again, which is one of the first signs you're getting clogged.

Whatever is in your life, is important to you. It's there for a reason. If it isn't, then why is it in your life? It's that simple. You're now equipped with sufficient self-awareness that keeps on growing, it's now up to you to use that knowledge.

ACTION

Everything you do can be reframed into a positive as you already know. As the wise and inspirational Mary Poppins used to say: *"In every job, there must be done, there is an element of fun, you find the fun… and snap, the job's a game."* But the simplest way to do so is to align it with your values, goals, and desires. This works instantly. Remember Ben? Who was struggling with all the demands of being a first-time father? As soon as he realised the most important value for him to uphold is supporting his wife— he felt motivated and excited to go to another baby's first birthday party.

That's why it's important for you to know your top values. When you feel you're struggling, go back to your values. And if you can't align it with your values, you might have to go back to the previous chapter and let go. It's our responsibility to choose the most empowering reasons for how we perceive and what we do in our lives.

I want to enjoy my work
I want to wake up with a smile on face
I want to feel I'm making a difference
I want to truly love my life

Before every important meeting or event, I set an intention for myself. Depending on the situation I will also voice this intention to the people involved. Every time my husband and I drive to our martial arts school we set an intention; something we want to focus on, bring to the foreground or actively work towards. By aligning your mind with a positive and inspirational goal, you equip yourself instantly, in a very simple and beautiful way.

Setting an intention is incredibly powerful, not only how it changes your perspective into feeling engaged and excited, but you're once again using the power of your mind. In a way, you're creating the outcome. You may have heard of the law of attraction (the famous book and movie *The Secret*), or using affirmations, shows using the power you have on a spiritual level. However, I'd like to explain it via the following research study. A group of Italian researchers (Bernardi et all, 2013) did a study with 16 pianists to practice a one-hand piano piece. They all had the same amount of daily time to practice over the course of one month. One group practiced while never touching a piano. A second group practiced as normal on the piano. And the third group combined physical and mental practice. Astonishingly, at the end of the study, the result of their performance of the piano piece did not differ that much. The use of the mind alone led to successful music learning. Using both physical and mental practice produced results that were indistinguishable from normal piano practicing.

Although this study involved quite a small group, we can understand that rehearsing something mentally can be really powerful, and if anything, at least beneficial. To set an intention and using the power of imagination, you're already one step ahead toward the achievement of your desired outcome.

What I love most about setting an intention is that it's giving you a directive, but still allowing space for other opportunities. A goal can be perceived as restrictive as it can set expectations; but an intention allows everything to unfold while staying clear on what to focus on. Be clear on your goal but remember to be open to the outcome.

Try it for yourself. The next time before you walk into a meeting, set an intention. Perhaps you want to ensure you don't react straight away, or let others be fully heard, or for you to gain clarity on the common goals. Whatever is important to you, your intention will help emphasise this.

Examine your options and choices with your goals and values in mind. And then do everything with the greatest intention and attention. Every thought you have, choice you make and action you take, is a direct reflection of how you want to live your life.

TIME TO UNCLOG

Hopefully, this all makes sense to you, but how to implement this in a practical way into your daily life? Here are my proven strategies.

- **Set daily intentions**: At the start of each day, set an intention for what you want to get out of the day. Briefly reflect at the end of the day whether that helped you.

- **Reframe your actions**: For the next week, when you feel like not doing something that you 'have to do'; reframe it so it becomes meaningful to you.

- **Change your approach**: If there's something you don't like doing, like housework or administrative tasks—make a list of why you like doing that task. If you are able to see the positive in it, you'll be able to approach it from an entirely different angle.

How does this support unclogging?

Aligning your actions with your beliefs is the essence of redoing, with the outcome that what you're doing has a purpose and feels light and adds value. This way it can never clog you up.

Decisions

The quality of decisions determines the quality of your life. But as there's so much going on in your life and the world around you, the quality of your decisions goes down if you make too many of them (decision fatigue). And if there are too many options, the quality of your decisions also goes down (confusion and overwhelm). We all make decisions differently, but we all use our rationale mind (the pre-frontal cortex) and our emotions (the amygdala), as described earlier on. As Daniel Kahneman in *Thinking, Fast and Slow* explains, while we'd like to think our decisions are rational, they're in fact mostly intuition driven. Thus, many happen without much consideration.

Think about decisions you've made that felt right; I guarantee you'll have a hard time explaining why you made that choice. Explaining it rationally will be challenging. For instance, the partner you chose, why did you select him/her? This might have been the biggest decision of your life, yet you didn't make it from your rational side. When we make decisions only based on facts and figures, using the rational part of your brain, as neuroscientist Richard Restak points out in his book *The Naked Brain*, we almost invariably end up 'overthinking'. We take longer to make decisions and they can end up being of lower quality. And with so many options out there, it makes us uncertain and this causes stress and anxiety. And even after the decision, you can still overthink whether it was the right one for you.

So, the more variables and input, the unhappier you'll be. Do you know the story of Hernán Cortés? In 1519 he led an expedition from Spain to Mexico and upon arrival, he ordered his men to burn the boats. His message was loud and clear: there's no turning back. We don't apply this enough in our own lives, we like to keep our options open. The 'just in cases', the 'what-ifs' and the 'howevers'. It's your responsibility to limit your options.

As described in Chapter 4, in Australia the cosmetic brand Head & Shoulders has 34 different shampoos and conditioners. And this brand holds 61 different selections in the USA. Research and product development teams continue providing us with new product selections every single day. But have you ever wondered whether you even need so many options? See, for me with my super short pixie cut, it doesn't matter much. I've found a natural cleanser that I wash my face, body, and hair with. Any hair product marketing falls on deaf ears to me. But that's because I've made a selective decision with regard to my hairstyle.

> In a complex world with abundant choices, we need good intuitions and smart shortcuts to make decisions.

Can you limit your options? Every action and every result start with a decision. There's no such thing as a free option, each decision costs mental energy and takes up time. To save you time, sanity and hopefully give you a better outcome, consider where you can filter some of the information. Perhaps you also want to wear one style of clothes like busy CEOs like Mark Zuckerberg and the late Steve Jobs. They made a conscious decision not to waste their energy on something that doesn't matter to them. Did you know that Barack Obama in his time in office only had two different coloured suits; grey or blue? It's for you to figure out what does and doesn't add value to you. Let's say you love your hair and it's part of making you feel great about yourself, then, of course, don't change it. But perhaps you can eat the same work lunch every day to make it easier for yourself. And please don't look for the options if you don't need it. I find the corporate lunch walk through the CBD malls 'the walk of not enough'. All the retailers compete for your attention to buy their product saying it'll make your life better; more comfortable, feeling sexier, being fitter, looking better. But what if we are already enough?

Besides the economic market, we also have more choices in our career, private life and even relating to our health. And all that information is readily available. It's not a matter of what's the best option out there, but what best fits your needs. Now is the time to match all the options in your environment to meet your individual needs.

In a complex world with abundant choices, we need good intuitions and smart shortcuts to make decisions. Ultimately, we must accept that uncertainty will always be part of what it is being human. But use your knowledge about yourself to prepare for your day and your future by ensuring you end up with the best decisions for yourself. Now that you are clear on who you are, what you believe in, what's important to you; you can apply this to any decision you make. Once you make this conscious decision, based on your values and what works for you, ensure you access and deal with the consequences. Don't wish for the situation to be different. This is your life, and if you fully accept your own decisions, it makes everything simpler.

TIME TO UNCLOG

Your life doesn't have to be as busy, complex and overwhelming. Let's focus on conscious decision making to simplify.

- **Reduce your choices**: What choices in your daily life could you reduce and are you willing to try? Just explore this, you've got nothing to lose and you can change it into a fun experiment.

- **Reflect at the end of the day**: Now you have this knowledge, you'll realise you'll become more aware of your options and decisions. At the end of the day, reflect on and identify one decision you now make more consciously with a different outcome than before.

ACTION

How does this support unclogging?

With the complexity of our world, we need to equip ourselves with tools to make decisions with better outcomes for ourselves. To filter out the options that don't provide any benefits are the effects of unclogging.

Unclog your communication

So far, we've only focused on you and how you interact with your physical and your own internal environment. But it's equally important to apply your knowledge to your relationships. Through learning about yourself, you'll also see your communication can and will improve. If, of course, you continue to apply what you know about yourself.

When we're clogged and under stress, we tend to react, not respond, be defensive and have less patience. Obviously, this is not conducive to effective communication. You'll act from a place of stress (fear response), rather than breathing deeply and staying calm. So, as you unclog, your relationships will also improve.

There's this Indian folktale about a bad-tempered snake in a village. The snake would terrorise the town and all the villagers were afraid of the snake. There have even been accounts of him biting the villagers. One day a sage visits the town and the villagers complain about the snake. The sage approaches the snake and tells him to stop terrorising the town; *"there's enough food, and there's no reason to attack"*. After a few weeks, the sage returns to the town and finds the snake all shrivelled up after being beaten with sticks by the villagers. The snake explains to the sage that he's taken his advice and he doesn't understand why they're all bullying him so much. The sage responds: *"Oh, foolish snake, I told you not to bite but I didn't tell you not to hiss."*

The same accounts for you. How you interact with the world is your choice. But it's a balancing act between being defensive and too compromising. Sticking to your guns also means that you can communicate it well in a way that supports you. If your close network is able to support you with what's important to you, then that grows tenfold. For the people that spend a lot of time with you, for them to understand your driving forces; your values and goals can be an absolute game changer. Think about it; do you remember Ben? He was struggling with the many first birthday parties he felt obliged to attend. In his case, if he could communicate to his wife what his values were and when he was then struggling with the situation, she could support him in making the right choice, or a shift in mindset. And of course, this goes vice versa in supporting her and her values. Plus, it's easier to support someone if they have clarity on their values themselves. It simplifies the entire situation.

Communication expert Michael Grinder taught me to communicate from a value perspective rather than behaviour. Your conversations and conflict resolutions, especially in your intimate relationship, will go much smoother. It's about understanding the values of the other person and what it means to them, rather than arguing to see who's 'right'. Now that you're clear on your values, it's important for you to apply them by helping others to understand you. Mutual understanding is the basis of effective communication. And to take it one step further; use the same inquisitiveness you've used with regard to yourself when trying to understand the other person. You are uniquely you, so is the other person. If you're able to see their perspective and broaden your view, your entire world will change.

Finally, the highlight of unclogged communication is having conversations with clarity and without distractions. Be present. If required, set rules for yourself to remove the distractions. Half an hour every day without devices to reflect on the day is something that has worked really well for me and my husband. It's also your responsibility to observe whether the other person isn't distracted. Ask them to put their phone away when they're ready or ask for a moment of their time as you've got something important to say. Be diligent and take ownership; if the conversation isn't going well, ask yourself what you can do differently.

The key is to be true to yourself, and also to others.

ACTION

Ask

'Ask' is one particular segment of communication I want to highlight here to wrap up this section. Jim Rohn pointed out to me in his book *Seven Strategies for Wealth and Happiness* that there's a command in the Bible that is essential to getting what you want and taking control: *"Ask, and you shall receive."*

Almost equally important as building your 'letting go' muscle and your capability to say 'no', is being able to ask for that what you want. And now you know clearly and exactly what you want, and your reasons for it, your confidence has also increased significantly.

I grew up never being afraid to ask what I wanted. Dates, trips, clothes, it didn't matter. My approach was rather pragmatic: I already knew I had a 'no' answer to begin with, so what did I have to lose?

I realise it does take a dose of courage to ask for what you need, but if you approach the other party with your request and explain what it means to you (and you will be able to clearly outline that), your part is done. If people understand your reasoning and purpose behind your request, they'll be much more willing to help as they now better understand where you're coming from. Approach it pragmatically and whatever the outcome, it's out of your control.

TIME TO UNCLOG

Being clear on what you want is a great feeling, but using that clarity to voice it to the people around really gives you the control of your life. It's a beautiful way to improve your relationships too.

- **Take ownership of how you communicate**: In the next week, identify areas where you could improve your communication through what you know about yourself. If you had a disagreement, reflect on it and see where you could have done better; were you focused/undistracted, were you clear on what you needed from the conversation or could you have tried harder to understand the other person's perspective?

- **Dare to ask**: Grow your 'willingness to ask' muscle. So many more opportunities will open up for you if you're daring to ask for that what you want or need.

How does this support unclogging?

Unclogging allows us to hold conversations without distractions and from the inside out. Applying what you know about yourself and taking control of your part of the conversation will result in effective communication.

ACTION

Spread positivity

In Chapter 6 we discussed the power of adding positivity, to find things that work for us rather than focussing on all else that may not work for us. Now you understand how to unclog your communication, being able to spread positivity is going to be even more powerful.

Studying the work of positive psychologists Shawn Achor and Martin Seligman, as described in Chapter 6, show that our level of happiness and enjoyment in life raises significantly as we not only seek for the positive aspects in our lives but also help others see that too. See, positivity spreads, negativity unfortunately also spreads. Think about you posting a vent or complaint on Facebook; you might receive criticism from people disagreeing, and you'll also receive applause from a lot of people agreeing with you and joining you in your frustration. I believe that it's important for us to vent and release a build-up of emotions, but I don't believe that a public space is the place for that (unless it has a very clear goal with a positive outcome for society). Be intentional and aware of what and how you are communicating.

Here is a list of what you can do to easily spread positivity:

- **Smile**: The simple act of sharing a smile does not only boost your mood but you'll see others smile back at you straight away.

- **Give a compliment**: It seems easier for us to complain rather than to acknowledge, but the easiest way of spreading positivity is to verbally share what you appreciate in others.

- **A random act of kindness**: If you see someone having a bad day, give them an extra dose of support. Helping someone is the most profound way to boost your own happiness as well as the happiness of others.

- **Ask different questions**: Instead of *"how was your day?"*, ask *"what was the highlight of your day?"* or *"what did you learn?"* Not only will you be the recipient of a more positive story, but it will also help the other party to see their day and life in a different light.

The effects of implementing these suggestions will work in the following ways:

- You are rewiring your brain, building your positive perspective and slowly eliminating your negativity bias.

- People will be drawn to your positive outlook and will be inspired by it.

- You'll make others happier and that will have a ripple effect in their lives.

In the beginning, this might be challenging for you, especially if you're new to this. But please remove that hesitation as these scientifically proven methods have the potential to make your life so much more joyful, grateful and meaningful.

ACTION

Do things differently

You now know so much more about yourself, it's now the time to put it all into action. For different results, we need to do things differently. As earlier on described as our powerhouse; our brain is capable of adapting and seeing our environment differently. It's now up to you to work towards an easier life, and continuously seeking what is working for you and what is not. And be real with yourself here; it's pointless to keep telling yourself the same self-sabotaging stories that are limiting you. Try new things.

We end up doing things we shouldn't, they affect us tremendously. How do I always end up on Facebook or YouTube when I grab my phone to send a text? We don't understand how it all works. But what does help, is to be alert and aware of it.

What are your distractions, your displacement activities? And what are your excuses? You don't have time to read 30 minutes every day but you're happy to binge watch Netflix over the weekend? You're saying you like being busy, yet you're always catching a cold? You're not feeling happy with your life, yet you're not actively working towards changing it?

Take responsibility for your life. The key to unclogging is to understand yourself and being able to apply it so you can take control of your environment rather than your environment taking control of you. Decide for yourself what it is you need to do. You have the capacity to change your entire life. Gain control over your days, actions, thoughts, and through that your entire life, rather than being controlled by them.

TIME TO UNCLOG

Being the catalyst for positivity isn't going to happen overnight. So, let's takes this in simple steps to start building on your capacity.

- **Acknowledge the people around you every day**: My husband and I have created a routine to acknowledge each other every day. It's so easy to get stuck in the negatives. Especially on those negative days, it's powerful to seek the positives and to share them with honesty and openness. Do this with your co-workers, your family, your friends; share with them why you appreciate them.

- **Challenge yourself**: What can you do differently that you're keen on really trying? Do you want to wake up earlier (I'd suggest reading *Morning Miracle* by Hal Elrod and your mornings will change forever) and consciously set yourself up for a great day? Are you keen to restrict your device use and implement the highly recommended one-hour analogue time after you wake up and before you go to bed, to limit your information consumption and start and finish the day from within and not controlled by your environment? Are you willing to lower the pressure on yourself by letting go of some requests or expectations, so you can focus on what matters most without feeling guilty?

How does this support unclogging?

Putting in the effort to spread positivity further eliminates your bias towards what isn't working. And if you are willing to do things differently to take control of your environment, you will unclog.

Key points

- Ensure everything you do has meaning. Start with intent.
- With too much going on in our lives, the quality of our decisions goes down. For a better result, we need to reduce our options.
- Use your self-knowledge to improve your communication, it's your decision how you interact with the world.
- Take responsibility to be the person you'd like to have around and have the willingness to do things differently.

Implementation

Create a new routine to support you with the forming of your new habits. To instil this, write down the following and implement it for the next three weeks:

- Set a daily intention.
- Compliment a person in your inner circle daily.
- Be fully present, that is without any disturbances when you have a conversation.
- And consider how you can reduce your options and try it.

Further learning

- Thinking, fast and slow - Daniel Kahneman
- The Art of Choosing - Sheena Iyengar
- Morning Miracle - Hal Elrod
- Happiness Advantage - Shawn Achor

PART IV
Review

This is the part of the process where you:

Pause, reflect and celebrate yourself

Learn to accept life is a challenge

Become aware that discipline and kindness is key

Commit to prioritising yourself

11

Stay unclogged

> *"Living gratefully begins with affirming the good and recognising its sources. It is the understanding that life owes me nothing and all the good I have is a gift."*
> – ROBERT EMMONS

Commit & celebrate

To stay unclogged it is essential to *review* — reassess where you're at, how far you've come and continue to adjust where necessary. For most people, this part of the process is the most vital aspect. If you miss this one, and you only focus on the rethinking and redoing part, you will end up feeling clogged again. To be your best self and live your best life, you need to take care of yourself.

What are you going to do, starting today, to take control of your life? Are you willing and committed to making a change? You might still be holding on to some of the stories and beliefs you have that are limiting you. Keep working on uncovering them. The key is to keep going. It's a practice. Trust

> You need to be in control but let go of your need to control.

yourself. Things will become easier. Remind yourself to view it differently, especially when you feel challenged.

With all the knowledge you now have, you understand a different and unclogged life is possible. You owe it to yourself to apply it and not to fall in the trap of self-sabotage again. You know what's right for you, no-one else can do this for you. You need to be in control but let go of your need to control. Take control of yourself and your environment. You can make your life less complicated. Commit to the process of unclogging; understand yourself — rethink; apply what you know — redo; and reassess and put yourself first — review.

Discipline creates simplicity

> Discipline will support you in creating your structure, kindness will support you in adapting when required. Discipline will teach you how to be ruthless with yourself, but it's just as important to be kind to yourself.

To continue making life work for you, there are two main habits you need to grow: discipline and kindness. Discipline will support you in creating your structure, kindness will support you in adapting when required. Discipline will teach you how to be ruthless with yourself, but it's just as important to be kind to yourself. Be ruthless in action, be kind in reflection. Don't confuse the two. You do need both. Build on both. Balance them both in a way that works for you, at the right time, and you'll be able to navigate through life with so much more ease.

Willingness comes before discipline. But by now I'm sure you're absolutely excited about your new perspective on life. Know that willingness and discipline will bring results. By setting new rules or routines for yourself, your life will automatically become simpler. When your mind is wandering and thinking of doing or focusing on other things, if you've made a set rule, stick to it. The same applies to the decisions you've made, stick to them. Discipline is aligning your actions with your goals. It's doing what you promised yourself you're going to do. Stop renegotiating. There will be a lot less noise in your mind, and it'll make your life a whole lot simpler.

Use your strengths to build your discipline. Exercising your strengths releases a positive emotion, plus it's the most efficient way for you to move towards your goals. Even if discipline isn't one of your strongest suits, don't be discouraged. You can utilise what you're naturally good at to build this skill. Are you good at learning? Then use studying to commit to your growth. Are you strategic? Then ensure you've got the right plan and strategy in place for you to succeed. Do what works for you.

Create a habit

Take it step by step. Don't overwhelm yourself and don't compare yourself to others. This is your life and we've already figured out your uniqueness, so align your amazing life with it. But make a daily commitment to yourself. EVERY day. Make it a ritual, a habit, build a routine to prevent you from going back to autopilot. Figure out the details. By just saying *"yes, I'll commit to checking in with myself every day"* you're setting yourself up for failure. When are you going to do it? How? Will you write it down and how are you going to commit?

Celebrate success

In our fast-paced society, where we run from one thing to the next in the blink of an eye, we have forgotten to celebrate how far we've come. When you're learning and progressing, it's important to celebrate your success. To relearn we need to reiterate. Celebrating, complimenting, or reflecting helps to rewire our brain. It helps to see the positives, to identify what we've already achieved, rather than focussing on all that isn't yet. You need to celebrate to keep going, it motivates, inspires and keeps you positive.

> **To relearn we need to reiterate.**

There is a difference between being successful and feeling successful—you could have achieved everything you hoped for and wanted, but it's important you feel it. Think back and appreciate what you have and celebrate your milestones, but most importantly bring it back to the core of you. What were your new goals, how are you going through your life day by day now versus a year or even a few months ago? How has it made your life easier?

You need to celebrate as it's a moment of reflection and helps you to actively seek out the positives of this journey you're on:

- **Be proud of yourself**: This helps you to build your belief in yourself. Your self-awareness is increasing, and you are making changes. You're doing things differently now and it's important to notice and celebrate the effects this has on you, your career, your health, and your relationships. Focus on the thoughts that build you up.

- **Notice your progress**: See the milestones, as small as they may seem. Not celebrating can have a huge effect on you getting clogged again as you're constantly striving for the next thing and not appreciating where you are and how far you've come.

- **It takes away overwhelm**: It simplifies the journey as it helps you see it isn't that overwhelming. You've reached some milestones; the road ahead looks shorter. If you don't reflect and celebrate your mind will still be thinking of the very long road ahead.

- **Celebrate life**: It amplifies your attitude of enough, it cultivates contentment. As Oprah states: *"The more you praise and celebrate your life, the more there is in life to celebrate."*

Commit to consciously taking in the amazingness of the life you have. It's magnificent, you've got everything you need right now and you're learning and growing. Be inspired by the journey and all the challenges you're overcoming.

TIME TO UNCLOG

How will you commit and work on building that habit? And remember to celebrate your milestones, you've come a long way.

- **Create a habit that works for you**: Grab your list of strengths and consider how you can best utilise them to create the routine that could work for you. You may have to adjust later on, but it's important you make a start. A routine makes life simpler as it reduces your options.

- **Don't delay celebrating**: Take some time this weekend to consciously celebrate yourself. Perhaps go for a nice long walk by yourself or perhaps go out with your partner, friends or kids. Ensure you put in the effort to reflect and see how far you've come already and notice how excited you'll feel to continue on this journey.

- **Celebrate to unclog**: When you feel you're getting clogged again, a celebration is one of the best remedies. It instantly brings about an attitude of enough and helps you see all the amazing things you've got going for you.

How does this support unclogging?

Being able to commit to yourself and celebrate will ensure you stay unclogged. You need to build yourself to have the energy to keep going and it all starts with putting yourself first.

Kindness

It's very important to be kind to yourself, it lowers the pressure you put on yourself. Be okay with where you're at, be okay not always doing things right and be okay with sometimes not feeling okay. As you learn to be kind to yourself, you'll be able to support yourself on an ongoing basis in what you need. And remember that there are only two thoughts you can have; it's thus better to focus on the ones that build you up. As Brian Tracy puts it: *"Never say anything about yourself that you do not want to come true."*

Here are several examples for you to learn to be nicer to yourself:

- **Learn to forgive yourself**: This is very important. Let go of resentment, guilt and that pressure to always be perfect.

- **Prioritise sleep**: Without sufficient rest, your body will automatically be more triggered into a stress response and that is a vicious cycle as you continue to deplete even more energy resources.

- **Recharge and prioritise yourself**: Take at least 10 minutes for yourself every day and work towards a block of time in the week (aim for two hours minimum) of doing something that invigorates you. Again, don't feel guilty for doing this, you need to recharge so you've got the motivation to continue.

- **Know what calms you**: Is it time for yourself or is it time for quality time with loved ones? Is it reading, playing a game or being in nature? This seems like a silly question, but we tend to get caught up so easily in what surrounds us, that we actually don't even know what really restores us. Become aware of your needs and what it is that brings you calmness.

- **Focus on yourself first**: Don't try to fix others first. Again, take ownership of your life and do what you need to do first. If you work on yourself, you can be the best version of yourself and only then will you be able to be the best partner, friend, parent or colleague there can be.

- **Give yourself permission to change**: Try new things and see if they work. Only then can you learn and adapt. But to succeed at this you have to give yourself permission to make mistakes, change your mind and not getting it right straight away.

- **Let go of the pressure**: Let go of self-imposed deadlines—it's okay to adjust. Let go of the pressure that you need to feel happy all the time—it's okay not to feel okay. Having empathy for oneself stops the cycle of getting clogged up.

By practicing self-compassion, you don't self-sabotage as you're kind and gentle with yourself and you see growth instead of failure, passion instead of pressure and recovery instead of non-productivity.

Interaction with others

Be kind to others. You need them on your journey. Even though the focus of unclogging is on you and your responsibility toward yourself, it ultimately results in how we interact with others. As we've already discussed in the previous chapter, you can spread positivity and you can communicate more clearly and with more understanding. Especially if others haven't caught up with your new approach yet; the level of intention and clarity you have now might be misunderstood as direct and forthright. Always aim to act with kindness, and that starts with understanding and being non-judgemental. Let go of the need to control others or the desire that they act in line with your expectations. They are on their journey and you are on yours. Support them, don't break them down. Here's a quick tip: say internally *"I understand"*, when you feel challenged by someone or frustrated with a situation. It's a simple yet effective way to create compassion. Plus, it helps you to straight away view it from another perspective, which we now know can change your entire life.

> **Treat yourself the way you would treat others and treat others the way you want to be treated.**

Treat yourself the way you would treat others and treat others the way you want to be treated.

TIME TO UNCLOG

Being kind is equally as important as being disciplined. Remember you need both, so take some time in this step to figure out what works for you.

- **Put yourself first**: How would that work best for you? What do you need to prioritise to have more energy on a daily basis? And how will you be able to accomplish it?

- **Be very mindful of how you speak of others and of yourself**: Aim to be kind and come from a place of understanding. It's challenging sometimes when we're in the heat of the moment but know that you can adjust your response at any moment.

How does this support unclogging?

Kindness lets go of so much internal pressure and is the basis for unclogging. The key to unclogging is to be in balance with your discipline and your kindness.

Reflection

To continue to learn we need to reflect. This way we can identify what's working and where we need or want to adjust. But as we've already identified, we're constantly busy scurrying from one thing to the next, without pausing and reflecting. Being able to stop is a habit we've unlearned.

Pause

We're losing our ability to just be. I remember from when I was a teenager back in the Netherlands, I would agree with a friend to meet in the morning so we could cycle to school together. I would stand there in the morning, waiting at a street corner wondering if I was too early or maybe too late. The only thing I could do was just standing there. How often do you see a person these days just standing somewhere and waiting? As soon as we have to wait for a bus, a train or a friend, we automatically grab our phones. We now have so many options and distractions to choose from, even when we don't need the distractions. It seems that we find comfort in all that noise.

I strongly feel that we're also losing our intuition because of this. Like, do we really need a fitbit telling us whether we had sufficient sleep? What if they came out with a chip implant that could tell your sugar or hormone levels at any time of the day? Yes, no doubt useful for a (pre) diabetic, but is that really data you want to process? And would it really be helpful for you?

Whether you agree or not, the fact is that we need time to digest the things we take in. Research by Manoush Zomodori shows that being bored is actually essential for our brain to process everything. In this time, it'll create the missing links, it'll store it, it'll see the bigger picture. If you're constantly taking in information, you won't be getting much use out of it in the long run. Without pausing you'll be less efficient. And this also fuels your behaviour towards constantly being on the go and perceiving you don't have enough time. It's the cycle of self-sabotage. Pausing is absolutely imperative for you to unclog and enjoy life to the fullest. We're naturally losing these moments, so you have to put in even more effort to stop this cycle.

Overcome rest resistance

It's important to stop viewing being busy, working hard and never taking sufficient downtime as something that's of benefit to you. What really is of benefit to you, even though you might not want to admit it, is to take a break. Schedule it in, commit to it and enjoy it without guilt. Going back to the point above that we need time to process, it's proven that you will be more productive when you do take those breaks. Not only will you get more done, but you'll also enjoy the process more. It'll be less draining (and you'll recover quicker) and you'll make fewer errors, so there will also be less 'fixing' to do. Way more efficient, right? It's entirely up to you, as always, to implement this, and I know it's hard, but I know you're reading this book because something isn't working for you and I'm only stating that you have the power to change it.

Overcome your habit to resist rest. Schedule time to do nothing.

Overcome your habit to resist rest. Schedule time to do nothing. The Italians have a beautiful saying for this: *Dolce Far Niente*, which roughly translates as the sweetness of doing nothing. Although I like the translation according to Merriam Webster more: pleasant relaxation in carefree idleness. Thomas Edison also knew the importance of this habit. He went fishing every day for an hour, and in his lifetime, he never caught any fish. The reason was that he never used any bait. When asked why not, he apparently responded; *"you don't get disturbed when you don't use any bait"*. Doing nothing for an hour every day clearly worked for one of the greatest inventors of our time.

Embrace stillness

I'd like to take doing nothing to the next level and discuss stillness. This is by far one of the most unappreciated aspects of our society. By incorporating stillness in your everyday life; it quietens the noise, it strengthens your understanding of yourself and it brings calmness. It is the most direct way to check in with yourself and being able to operate from within, rather than letting the outside dictate your actions, thoughts, and feelings. It stops the analytical mind and helps you see things from a different perspective.

Being still is simple, but not easy. It's very challenging to sit down and not react. There are actually three levels of silence: the first one is no sound (this one is obvious), the second is no movement (stillness of the body) and the final level is no thoughts (stillness of the mind). By bringing more stillness into your life you do not have to aim for those three levels at the same time, but it's merely for your awareness and understanding that becoming quiet has different graduations. Ultimately, the most beneficial is the silence in the mind: there are no more questions buzzing, all the noise has gone, what's left is silence.

As you're aiming to implement more stillness, it's important not to resist it, but get excited about silence. Know how it can benefit your psychological state, but also savour the moment and resist the urge to get up and do something. Be okay with being alone, which is another useful skill to have. Blaise Pascal wisely pointed out; *"All of humanity's problems stem from man's inability to sit quietly in a room alone."* And I believe he's right. Your mind is always busy, it has control over you with its endless source of distractions, restlessness, fear, and worries. But once you sit still with all your mind chatter and become aware of these thoughts that jump up almost out of nowhere, you will see that they dissipate and lose their power. Try sitting down for 5 minutes, you can even set a timer. See how often you feel the need to get up and do something. Your mind will even prompt you to get up by saying 'in case you forget'. But notice what happens if you don't get up. It's all okay and the thought might even disappear.

Bringing stillness and more non-doing into your life is a challenging tool to implement, but it has a profound effect on how you interact with your environment. It will reaffirm your self-awareness and will cultivate the three C's: confidence, compassion, and contentment.

TIME TO UNCLOG

Bringing in time to reflect is such a hard one for most people to implement and sometimes we need to keep reminding ourselves of it. Try it, realise the benefits, and invest in yourself.

- **Schedule time to do nothing**: Or at least aim to do nothing for several moments of your day.

- **Take time for yourself**: Take time out when the situation calls for it; if you notice yourself overreacting, feeling overwhelmed or not like yourself.

- **Practice silence**: For at least two weeks, sit all alone in silence every day for 5 minutes. See what comes up and resist the urge to get up.

- **Meditate if you're ready for it**: Morning or evenings are best, it's easier as your mind will most likely be calmer. Don't try to meditate when you're overwhelmed or frustrated, this will only work against you. The simplest method is to sit cross-legged or in a chair with your spine straight, eyes closed while observing your breathing. When your mind wanders, just bring it back to the breathing.

How does this support unclogging?

Through reflection, you are able to identify and adjust what isn't working. It aids in breaking the cycle of self-sabotage. Through pausing, and doing nothing, we can restore ourselves which provides us the energy to deal with everything that comes our way.

Reality

So, we've covered a lot and hopefully, you've been able to apply most of this as you've worked through the book. Or at least you're now fully ready to apply the three steps of **rethink, redo** and **review**, that will help you go through life with so much more ease. Life doesn't have to be this complicated; if we take ownership and unclog our minds and our environment, it will go much smoother.

But a reality check is necessary; we will get clogged again. Life does that, but you now have the tools to work on it and apply it on an ongoing basis so you can eliminate the disruptors. It's key to embrace reality; not wishing things to be different will bring you more happiness.

Disruptors and indicators

Going back to the kitchen sink analogy in Chapter 4 to outline the principle of unclogging; it's important to know what gets your sink clogged. What gets you clogged may not affect me at all, so it's up to you to figure out what your disruptors are. Once you have that awareness, you'll be able to act more promptly to solve them.

In line with that, it's also helpful to identify your indicators for being clogged. What is your auto-response behaviour when life isn't going well for you? Being clear on these triggers will help you manage the situation and reduce the risk of even getting clogged in the first place.

For me, for a long time, I would get clogged by comparing myself to others, but in more recent times the biggest challenge for me is being impatient and putting high expectations on myself, especially self-imposed deadlines. My indicators haven't really changed; I react snappily, have less tolerance for people and I'm not my enthusiastic and positive self.

Build a solid foundation for yourself

By doing this work and going through the three steps of unclogging, you will have created a foundation for yourself. And when life gets more challenging, you've got your toolkit to use. It creates your stability, so you can feel not only in control, but you can also adapt to your ever-changing environment. The key is having both a sufficient structure and flexibility, like a tree. Continue learning about yourself, because you'll evolve too. And as you grow, so will your understanding of yourself. Even though you have a stable foundation, remind yourself you're not a fixed entity. Focus on what you can control, and adapt when you need or want to.

And realise that even slow change is change. It might sometimes feel you're taking five steps back, but if you in all honesty and with a dose of positivity assess your progress, you'll realise you've definitely come a long way. Just because things get challenging again, and you might even get clogged again, it may not be as bad as before. And I'm absolutely certain you'll be able to deal with it more swiftly, so it doesn't affect you as much.

If you've had a challenging time or you've had to act out of alignment with what works best for you, it's important you recover quickly. This is where you've overused your energy in your sympathetic nervous system, so it's important for you to reduce your stress levels to improve your wellbeing. Create as many moments to recover as possible. Perhaps it might be taking outside lunch breaks or working in a closed and quiet office for a few hours in the afternoon, but ensure you take care of what you need, even though that may be after the fact. Use your toolkit for this, as described in the next chapter.

There is no solution, no quick fix. It's a matter of you building your stable and solid foundation and then being flexible enough to adapt to your surroundings. By finding the balance between those two states, you can take control of your environment, rather than your environment taking control of you. That's unclogging.

TIME TO UNCLOG

As you're coming to end of all this and you've made so much progress, it's important you can continue staying unclogged.

- **Know your disruptors and indicators**: List what you think could be your disruptors and indicators. Add them to the list of your collation of your self-knowledge; your strengths, values, etc. from Chapter 5. Now you are aware of them, you're able to sooner identify them arising, so you can also act more swiftly.

- **Take a deep breath**: We've come to the end of all this, and you've learned a lot. Take some time to process it and let it sink in. Relax and take a deep breath. You've got this.

How does this support unclogging?

The process of unclogging is cyclic and requires ongoing work. But being aware and in acceptance of the reality that your drain will get clogged again, is the most helpful attitude to have so you can be prepared to deal with the issues as they arise.

Key points

- The cyclic process of unclogging requires an ongoing commitment.
- Celebrating your progress is key to staying motivated.
- You need to know which moments require discipline or kindness.
- Doing nothing and being still is paramount to your personal growth.

Implementation

Set your routine in line with what works for you:

- Practice silence every day.
- Keep discovering what works for you.
- Become aware of your disruptors and indicators.

Further learning:

- Extreme Ownership - Jocko Willink
- Quiet - Susan Cain
- Untethered Soul - Michael Singer

12

What's next

Build your toolkit

Now you understand how the process of unclogging works, and you're aware that you can and will get clogged again. The process of rethink, redo and review is a cyclic process and you'll continue learning more about yourself, what works for you and being able to implement that.

The next step is to stay unclogged. By paying attention to your indicators and disruptors, as you've identified in the previous chapter, you can avoid the impact of what life throws at you, or at least minimise it. By understanding what doesn't work for you, or how you behave when you get clogged, you'll be able to do something about it. This way you can adjust your situation, ask for help, let go, say no, or any of the other actions that are suitable at that stage.

But to really stay unclogged, the most important thing you can do for yourself is build your toolkit. That's how you can take care of your drain. Figure out whether you need a 'strainer' or some 'chemicals'. You know your drain best. Become your own plumber.

We've already identified some tools that work for you and perhaps some of them you've already been doing or started implementing. Fantastic! This toolkit is essential as it holds the actions that work for you. Whether it's no phone one hour before and after sleeping, no sugar in your diet, meditation or something as simple as going for a walk or giving away a compliment. We can all make suggestions, but you need to figure out and apply what works for you. I can't decide that for you, only you can. But of course, you need to be willing to try different things, for different results.

Take journaling; for me, it's something I really don't feel like. I know it has so many merits and I admire people that consistently do so, however for me it always feels like a chore and something I have to do. I did really try, but it's not working for me. So, I'm not doing it. What I do do, is I reflect on the day with my husband through a 10 to 20-minute conversation where we openly talk about our day, our highlights and our challenges. It's quality time and as we're both doing our own thing for many hours of the day, that tool works for me.

Remember we've talked briefly about meditation; well if you're not ready for it, or it feels like a chore to you, I'd be the last one that would recommend it to you. I do know we all need some pauses and moments of stillness in our day, but it's up to you to figure out how you want to incorporate it. So, take any element from this book and see how you can make it work for you. It should align with you, not work against you. And of course, you can always try. Give it a go, reflect on whether it worked for you, and if it does, add it to your arsenal.

The toolkit you're building is there to support you. The tools help to bring out the best in you, to stay in your optimum mode of operating, and they make sure you can handle the disruptions, the noise, and the overwhelm.

Write them down

To really become the captain of your own ship you need to write these tools down. As you're trying them out (preferably one by one, for about three weeks to start with) but especially as you're realising that they are essential for you, list them.

See, it's your job to apply your knowledge consistently. But in reality, we forget what works for us. We take our own knowledge for granted; we don't think it's that valuable, we don't implement it and we sometimes even forget about it. It may sound ridiculous, or just for forgetful people, but research shows, all beautiful compilated in Atul Gawande's book *The Checklist Manifesto,* when we are in a stressful situation, we will forget the most basic supportive actions, and that's when we need them most. Faulty memory and distractions play a role in us forgetting these important tasks. See the checklist you're building as a cognitive safety net. You're creating the structure you can rely on when the wind blows. It's a simple system that can equip you to manage everyday life and future challenges. In the complexity of our world, we must do something different, a simple checklist might do the trick.

When life gets challenging or overwhelming, the easiest way for you to simplify it and make it work for you is by going back to your checklist. To apply techniques and tools when you need them, that is wisdom. And if you don't, that's when you sabotage yourself. Take control of this by making your checklist. It's like making an agreement with yourself as to how you'll ensure to take care of yourself. How you can be your best self and make life easier for yourself.

TIME TO STAY UNCLOGGED

Let's start building your toolkit. And continue working on it; through using it, reassessing and adjusting it.

- **List what you already do and what you want to try**: Write a list of the techniques you already use but sometimes forget to use them. And make a second list of new ones you'd like to start implementing. Try to keep it simple—between 5-9 items so you can easily memorise them, as you need to know what to use in the more challenging moments.

- **Keep your list safe**: Have the list with you and remind yourself to use it. Perhaps have it on your phone in notes or in an app like Trello. This list is your safety net with all the wonderful tools that work for you, it's uniquely you and they're your proven strategies.

- **Reflect on this list occasionally**: This is your own first aid box, but it also works preventatively. So, keeping it up to date is essential.

How does this support unclogging?

Unclogging is all about uncovering what works for you. Building your own toolkit is the most efficient way of taking care of yourself as you implement what you know about yourself. It's your answer to how you manage yourself and anything that comes your way. Your antidote to overwhelm.

For organisations

The process of unclogging also applies to how we can run our organisations more efficiently. The same principle of working from the inside out applies here. There is so much noise out there, that it's vital for any organisation to be clear on their values, goals, and uniqueness. And then it shouldn't be only written in a filed away document; it needs to be communicated clearly and precipitated through all levels and seen in everything that's done. Ensure the company values are clearly outlined and are cascaded from the top down. All employees need to be able to align with these values so they can apply the unclogging cycle to ensure the organisation flows.

And on an individual level for each employee applying what works for them makes the organisation more efficient as unclogged workers are:

- **Happier**: When people get to use their strengths on a daily basis and they know they can use them to contribute to the company's mission, their engagement and job satisfaction increases, resulting in higher staff retention and team morale improves.

- **More efficient**: As they know what works for them and they're able to implement this with confidence and clarity, they're not wasting energy on something that doesn't come naturally.

- **More resilient**: When people are clear on their foundation, and they're able to take care of their needs, they're much more capable to adapt when required.

- **More compassionate**: Being able to fully understand your uniqueness, will allow you to also see the uniqueness in others. As you know what works for you, you'll be trying to find that in others too. It's a ripple effect.

As we've discussed ecosystems in this book to explain the importance of being in balance, the same applies to an organisation. All elements can operate in balance, but even when it's not, having a solid foundation will ensure balance can be restored quickly.

An organisation will benefit when applying this process by:

- Aligning and actioning core values, goals and mission.

- Being able to deal with disruptions through a supportive team morale.

- Growing their influence as market leaders as clear communication can flow through from the inside out.

About the author

Simplicity Expert Eve Broenland is dedicated to helping individuals rise above the overwhelm of modern life and simplify their environment from the inside out.

Referred to as the antidote to overwhelm, Eve's pragmatic three-step process known as 'Unclogging' has helped individuals all over the world streamline their life, become more decisive and confidently create the best version of themselves.

Her Dutch heritage naturally makes her approach clear and direct. Her double Masters Degree in Environmental Science and Marine Biology has taught her to see how disruptions affect our lives. She also is a qualified traditional yoga teacher, co-owns a martial arts school and has extensively researched eastern philosophy, positive psychology and minimalism.

Having struggled with the overwhelm of daily life herself, Eve delivers simple, systematic and practical advice in a personable way. As a speaker, facilitator and coach her clients praise her for her encouraging positivity, clear approach and valuable insights.

Eve resides in suburban Perth in a lovely home with a minimal interior together with her husband and two dogs.

www.evebroenland.com

References

Chapter 4
Barry Schwartz, *The Paradox of Choice* (2005, July) [video file]. Retrieved from https://www.ted.com/talks/barry_schwartz_the_paradox_of_choice

Sheena Iyengar, *The Art of Choosing* (USA: Abacus, 2011)

Chapter 5
Donald Clifton & Paula Nelson, *Soar With Your Strengths* (USA: Dell, 1995)

Gay Hendricks, *The Big Leap* (USA: HarperCollins Publishers Inc, 2010)

Louise Hay, *You Can Heal Your Life* (USA: Hay House Inc, 2008)

Amy Cuddy, *Your Body Language May Shape Who You Are* (2012, June) [video file]. Retrieved from https://www.ted.com/talks/amy_cuddy_your_body_language_may_shape_who_you_are

Jordan Peterson, *12 Rules for Life* (Great Britain: Penguin Books Ltd, 2018)

Mihaly Csikszentmihalyi, *Flow* (USA: HarperCollins Publishers Inc, 2008)

Danielle LaPorte, *The Desire Map* (Australia: Sounds True Inc, 2019)

REFERENCES

Chapter 6
Bruce Lipton, *Biology of Belief* (USA: Hay House Inc, 2016)

Barry Neil Kaufman, *Son Rise* (California: H J Kramer, 1995)

Shawn Achor, *Before Happiness* (United Kingdom: Virgin Books, 2013)

Hans Rosling, *Factfulness* (London: Sceptre Books, 2019)

Dr. Martin Seligman, *Authentic Happiness* (London: Nicholas Brealey Publishing, 2002)

Dr. Kazuo Murakami, *The Divine Code of Life* (New York: Beyond Words Publishing, 2006)

Chapter 7
Tim Ferriss, *Why You Should Define Your Fears Instead Of Your Goals* (2017, April) [video file]. Retrieved from https://www.ted.com/talks/tim_ferriss_why_you_should_define_your_fears_instead_of_your_goals

Dr. Andrew Newberg & Mark Robert Waltman, *Words Can Change Your Brain* (New York: Penguin Group, 2013)

Debi Roberson, Jules Davidoff, Ian Davies & Laura Shapiro (2006) *Colour categories and category acquisition in Himba and English*, Progress in Colour Studies: Volume II. Psychological aspects. John Benjamin Publishing Company.

Dr Masaru Emoto, *Hidden Messages in Water* (New York: Atria Books, 2005)

Chapter 8

Erik Helzer & Shai Davidai (2016) *The Cult of Busy*, John Hopkins Health Review. Retrieved from https://www.johnshopkinshealthreview.com/issues/spring-summer-2016/articles/the-cult-of-busy

Dan Pontefract, *You Are Way Too Busy; It's Hampering Your Ability To Think And Be Productive* (2018, July) [Article]. Retrieved from https://www.forbes.com/sites/danpontefract/2018/07/09/you-are-way-too-busy-its-hampering-your-ability-to-think-and-be-productive/#7eea1528a4cc

Wayne W. Dwyer, *Excuses Begone!* (USA: Hay House Inc, 2009)

Chapter 9

Patrick Rhone, *Enough* (Kindle Edition, 2016)

Brene Brown, *The Gifts of Imperfection* (Minnesota: Hazelden Publishing, 2010)

Joshua Becker, *The More of Less* (Colorado: Waterbrook Press, 2016)

Chapter 10

Bernardi et all (2013) *Mental practice promotes motor anticipation: evidence from skilled music performance*, Frontiers in Human Neuroscience. Retrieved from https://www.ncbi.nlm.nih.gov/pmc/articles/PMC3747442/

Daniel Kahneman, *Thinking, Fast and Slow* (UK: Penguin Books, 2011)

Richard Restak, *The Naked Brain* (New York: Crown Publishing, 2006)

Jim Rohn, *Seven Strategies for Wealth and Happiness* (Melbourne: Brolga Publishing, 2007)

REFERENCES

Chapter 11
Manoush Zomorodi, *How Boredome Can Lead To Your Most Brilliant Ideas* (2017, April) [video file]. Retrieved from https://www.ted.com/talks/manoush_zomorodi_how_boredom_can_lead_to_your_most_brilliant_ideas

Chapter 12
Atul Gawande, *The Checklist Manifesto* (New York: Metropolitan Books, 2009)

Acknowledgments

A big thank you to the following people:

Dianne McCabe, Sue Lindsay and Sharon Muscet for supporting me in writing this book. You always have my back and I can count on you for input, support and honesty. Without your encouragement and unwavering belief in me, this book wouldn't have been possible.

Sam Cawthorn for showing me this is possible, but mostly your trust in me so I could back myself. Warren Tate for your friendship, laughs and support since the day we met. Nick Harding for his fantastic idea and helping me bring it to you. Jessica Kiely for endorsing this idea thereby instilling it in my mind.

Rosie and Quentin, thank you for letting me stay at your beautiful place for undisturbed writing time in nature.

To my editor Johanna Leigh for your invaluable contribution, my designers May Phan and Marvin Tojos for packaging it up so perfectly.

My wine club ladies for always believing in me.

My parents and brother, my sincere thanks for being there for me since the day I came to this world. We live on different continents but nonetheless, we're there for each other.

ACKNOWLEDGMENTS

To my husband; Frank you are my rock, you supported me during the challenging years, but in a way that I was able to explore what I needed. You never have any doubt in me and that means everything to me. You were proud of me before I even started.

To all my clients, past, present and future; I learn so much from you and it's because of your trust in me I'm able to do what I love. I feel honoured to work with you and I'm always beyond excited when I see you apply what you've learned about yourself. Unclogging your life is what drives me every day.

Lastly, I want to thank myself; for my determination, my inner drive to make an impact, to fully utilise all my skills, talents and knowledge to make people's lives more simple. To constantly learn and challenge myself, to walk my talk and implement what I've learned, and to have the courage to grow into a person who can make a difference.